SPACE DOGS

TIM FURNISS

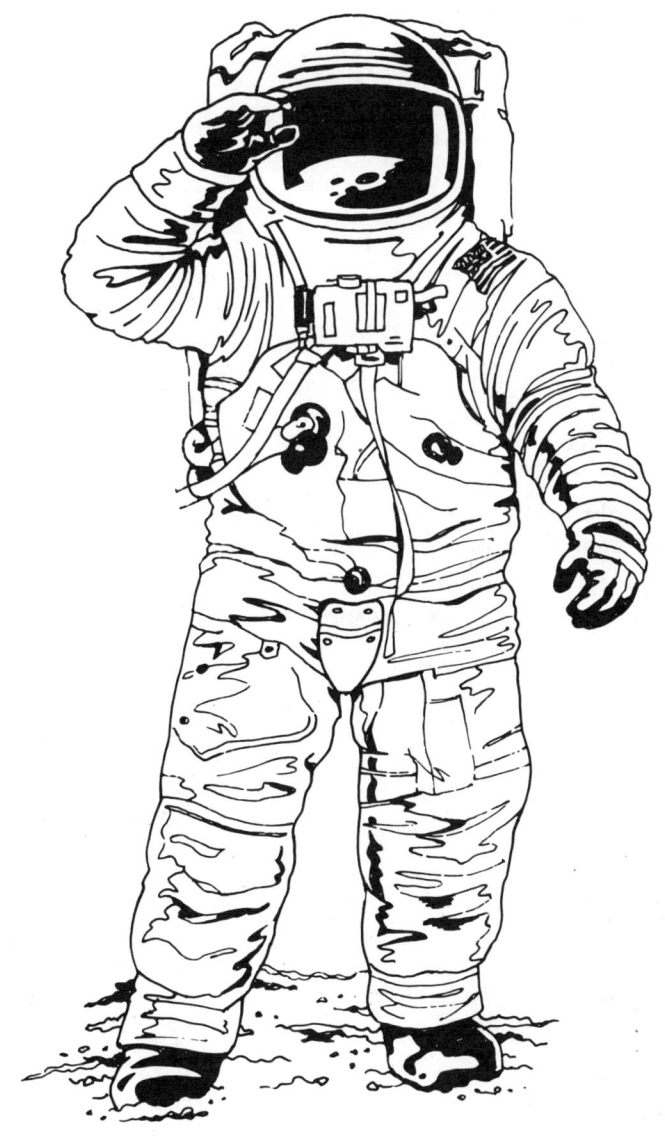

SIMON & SCHUSTER
LONDON • SYDNEY • NEW YORK • TOKYO • TORONTO

First published in Great Britain by
Simon & Schuster Limited 1989

Text and illustrations copyright © Eddison Sadd Editions 1989
This edition copyright © Eddison Sadd Editions 1989

This book is copyright under the Berne Convention.
No reproduction without permission. All rights reserved.

Simon & Schuster Limited, West Garden Place,
Kendal Street, London W2 2AQ

Simon & Schuster Australia Pty Limited
Sydney, New South Wales

ISBN 0 671 69713 7

AN EDDISON SADD EDITION
Edited, designed and produced by
Eddison Sadd Editions Limited
St Chad's Court, 146B King's Cross Road,
London WC1X 9DH

Phototypeset by Bookworm Typesetting,
Manchester, England
Produced by Mandarin Offset in Hong Kong

WHAT TO DO

Welcome to SPACE DOTS.
Here's how you can learn about rockets, shuttles, satellites and spacemen and spacewomen. This is your mission ...

❶ Find a soft pencil or a black, felt-tipped pen.
❷ Choose a puzzle.
❸ Find the start of the puzzle – there is a little arrow on the puzzle to help you find dot number 1.
❹ Join up the dots in the correct order.
❺ What does your space picture show?
❻ Now look at the sticker sheet.
❼ Find the correct sticker for your picture. Sometimes a line has been traced inside the outlined shape, or you will be able to recognise the picture.
❽ Place the sticker over the dotted outline.
❾ Colour in your picture.
❿ Answer the quiz box questions by putting a tick in the box of your choice. (Sometimes the sticker will give you a clue.) You can check your answers in the back of the book.
⓫ Count up all your points and see if you are a GALACTIC SPACE ACE!
⓬ Complete your mission by copying the name of the puzzle, from the answer, into the spaces under the quiz box questions.

THE SPACE AGE

We have always dreamed of exploring space. This was not possible until large enough rockets were developed in 1957. In that year, a Russian rocket launched the first satellite into orbit around the Earth. The Space Age had begun. During the first years of the Space Age, there was a tremendous competition between Russia and America to be first to achieve each new target in space exploration. This was called the Space Race. Some great moments in the Space Race were: when the first craft reached the Moon (1959); when the first man was sent into space (1961); and, eventually, when the first man walked on the Moon (1969). The 1960s period was a very exciting time in which to follow developments in space. Today, we have learned to use space to improve life on the Earth, using many kinds of satellites for communications. Both America and Russia have built reusable spacecraft, called shuttles, which can fly into space and back, rather like aircraft. Space stations have been launched, and new ones are planned. Many spacecraft are being sent towards the planets, comets and asteroids, to continue our exploration of space.

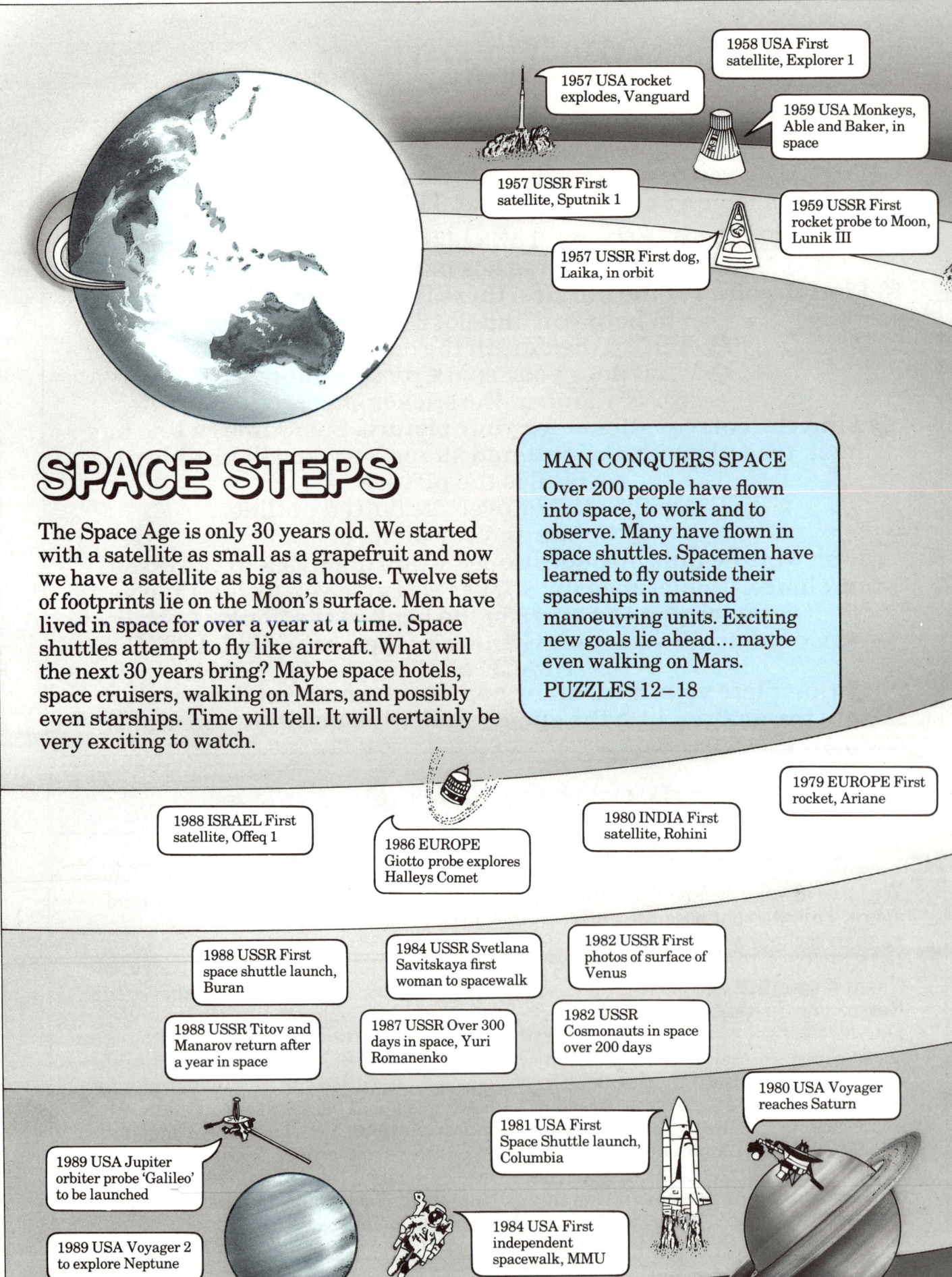

SPACE STEPS

The Space Age is only 30 years old. We started with a satellite as small as a grapefruit and now we have a satellite as big as a house. Twelve sets of footprints lie on the Moon's surface. Men have lived in space for over a year at a time. Space shuttles attempt to fly like aircraft. What will the next 30 years bring? Maybe space hotels, space cruisers, walking on Mars, and possibly even starships. Time will tell. It will certainly be very exciting to watch.

MAN CONQUERS SPACE
Over 200 people have flown into space, to work and to observe. Many have flown in space shuttles. Spacemen have learned to fly outside their spaceships in manned manoeuvring units. Exciting new goals lie ahead... maybe even walking on Mars.
PUZZLES 12–18

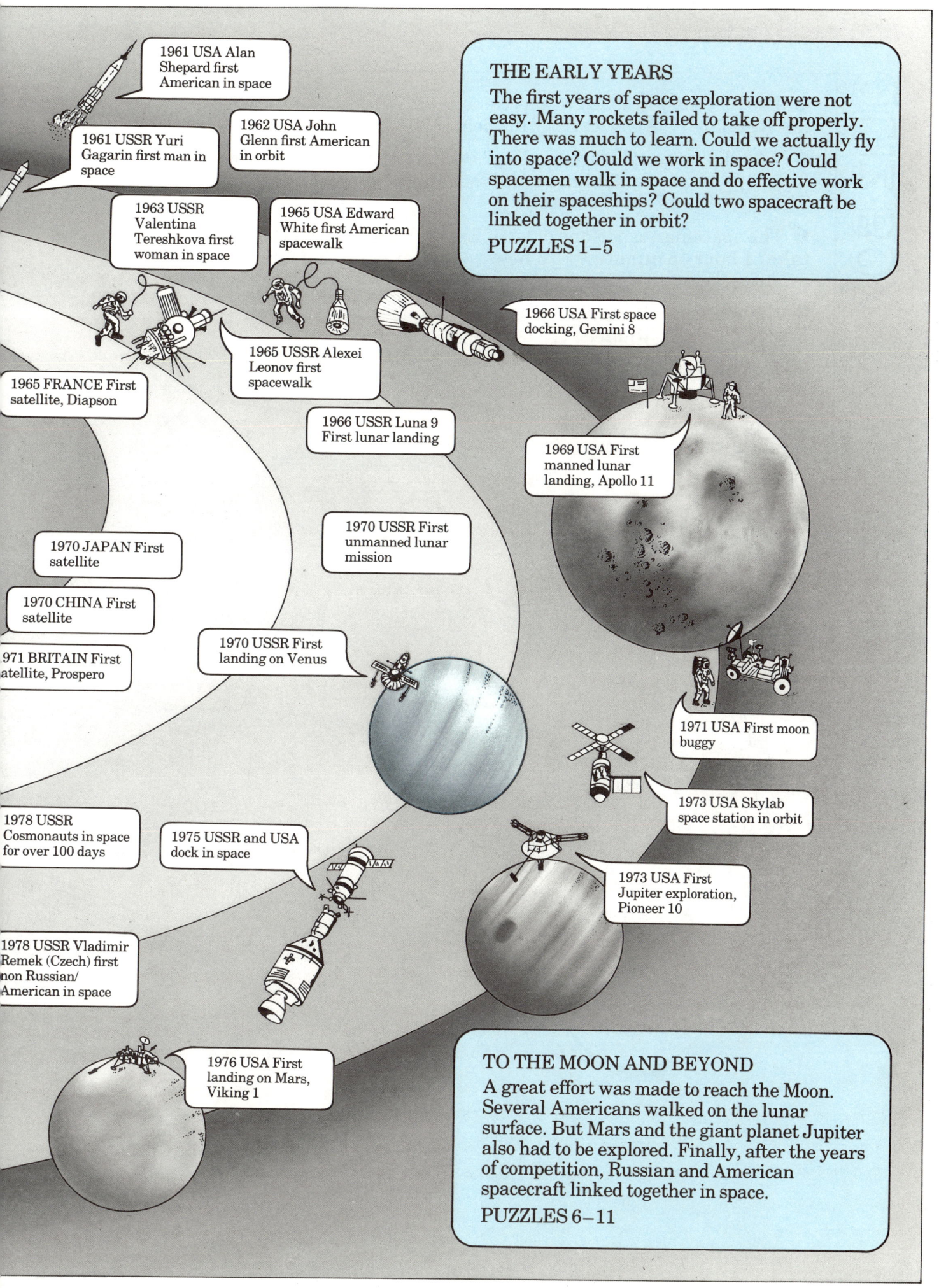

QUIZ BOX 1

❶ The first man in space was a cosmonaut. What nationality was he? Russian? ☐ American? ☐ French? ☐

❷ Why did he eject before landing? Because the capsule's parachute failed? ☐ He would not have survived landing inside? ☐ The capsule was out of control? ☐

❸ The spaceman made one orbit of Earth. How long did the flight take? 1 hour 48 minutes? ☐ 3 hours 47 minutes? ☐ 5 hours 5 minutes? ☐

❹ His spacecraft was called Vostok. What does Vostok mean? East? ☐ West? ☐ Sunrise? ☐

Spaceman's name ☐☐☐☐
☐☐☐☐☐☐☐

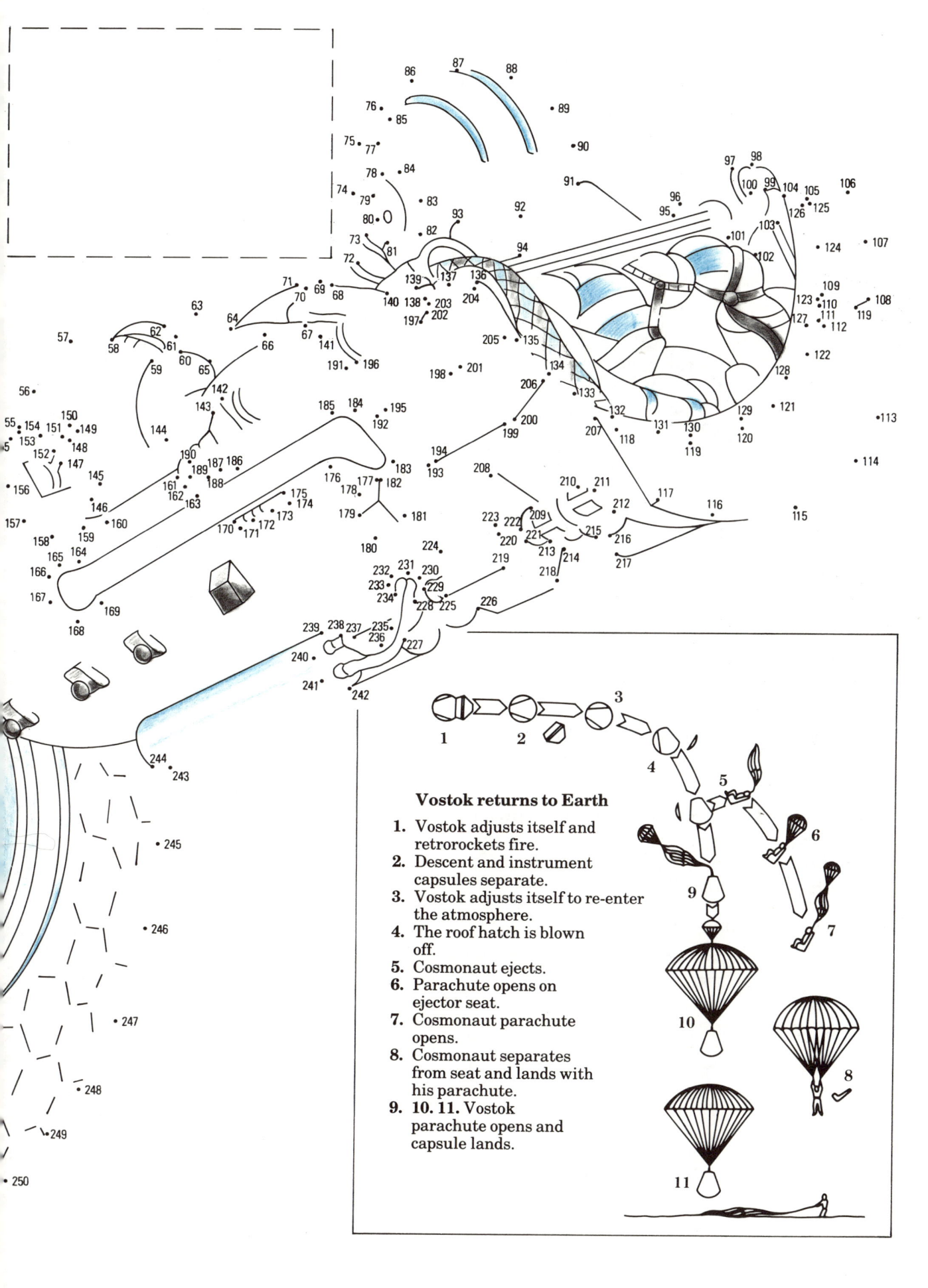

Vostok returns to Earth

1. Vostok adjusts itself and retrorockets fire.
2. Descent and instrument capsules separate.
3. Vostok adjusts itself to re-enter the atmosphere.
4. The roof hatch is blown off.
5. Cosmonaut ejects.
6. Parachute opens on ejector seat.
7. Cosmonaut parachute opens.
8. Cosmonaut separates from seat and lands with his parachute.
9. 10. 11. Vostok parachute opens and capsule lands.

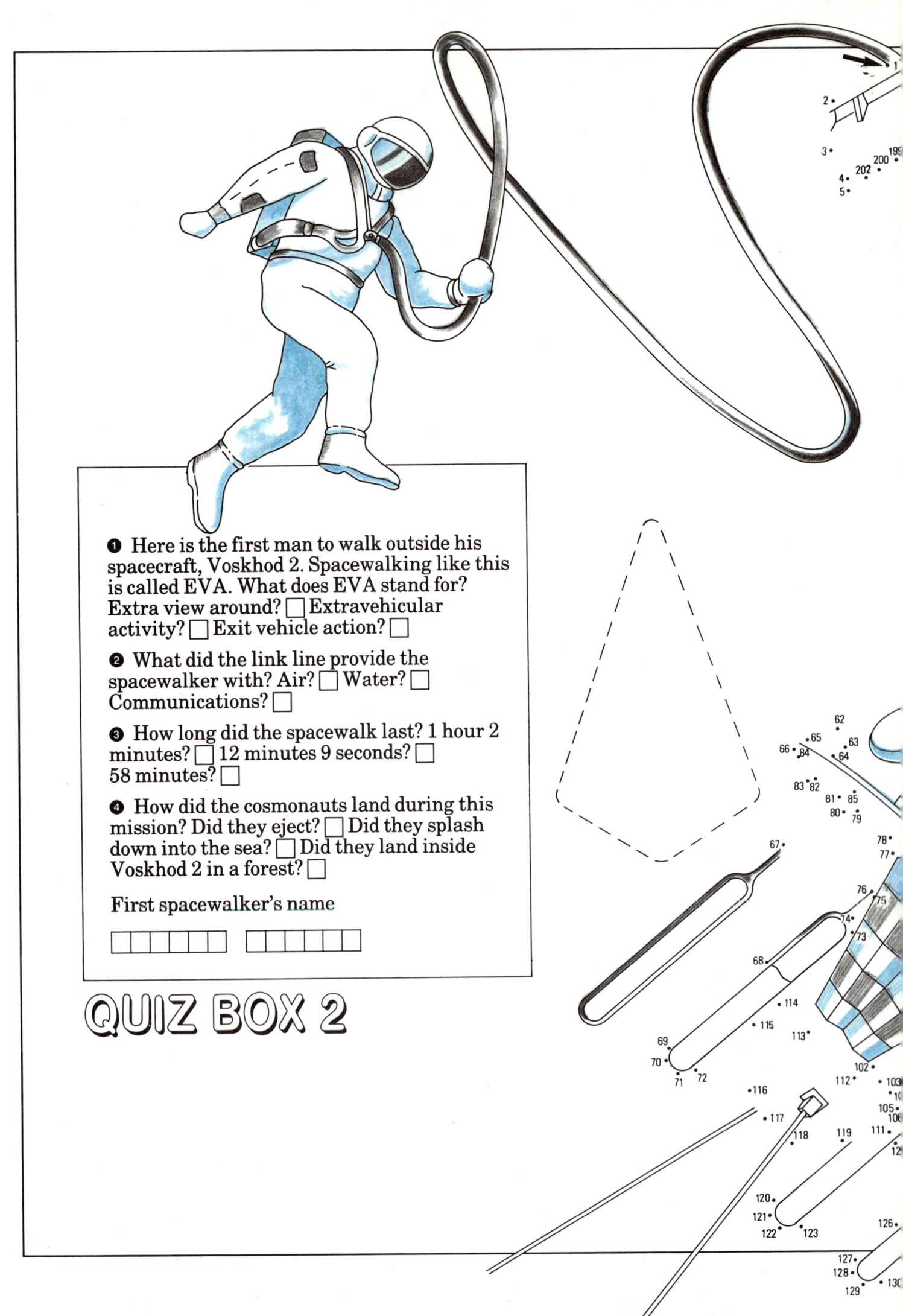

❶ Here is the first man to walk outside his spacecraft, Voskhod 2. Spacewalking like this is called EVA. What does EVA stand for? Extra view around? ☐ Extravehicular activity? ☐ Exit vehicle action? ☐

❷ What did the link line provide the spacewalker with? Air? ☐ Water? ☐ Communications? ☐

❸ How long did the spacewalk last? 1 hour 2 minutes? ☐ 12 minutes 9 seconds? ☐ 58 minutes? ☐

❹ How did the cosmonauts land during this mission? Did they eject? ☐ Did they splash down into the sea? ☐ Did they land inside Voskhod 2 in a forest? ☐

First spacewalker's name

☐☐☐☐☐ ☐☐☐☐☐☐

QUIZ BOX 2

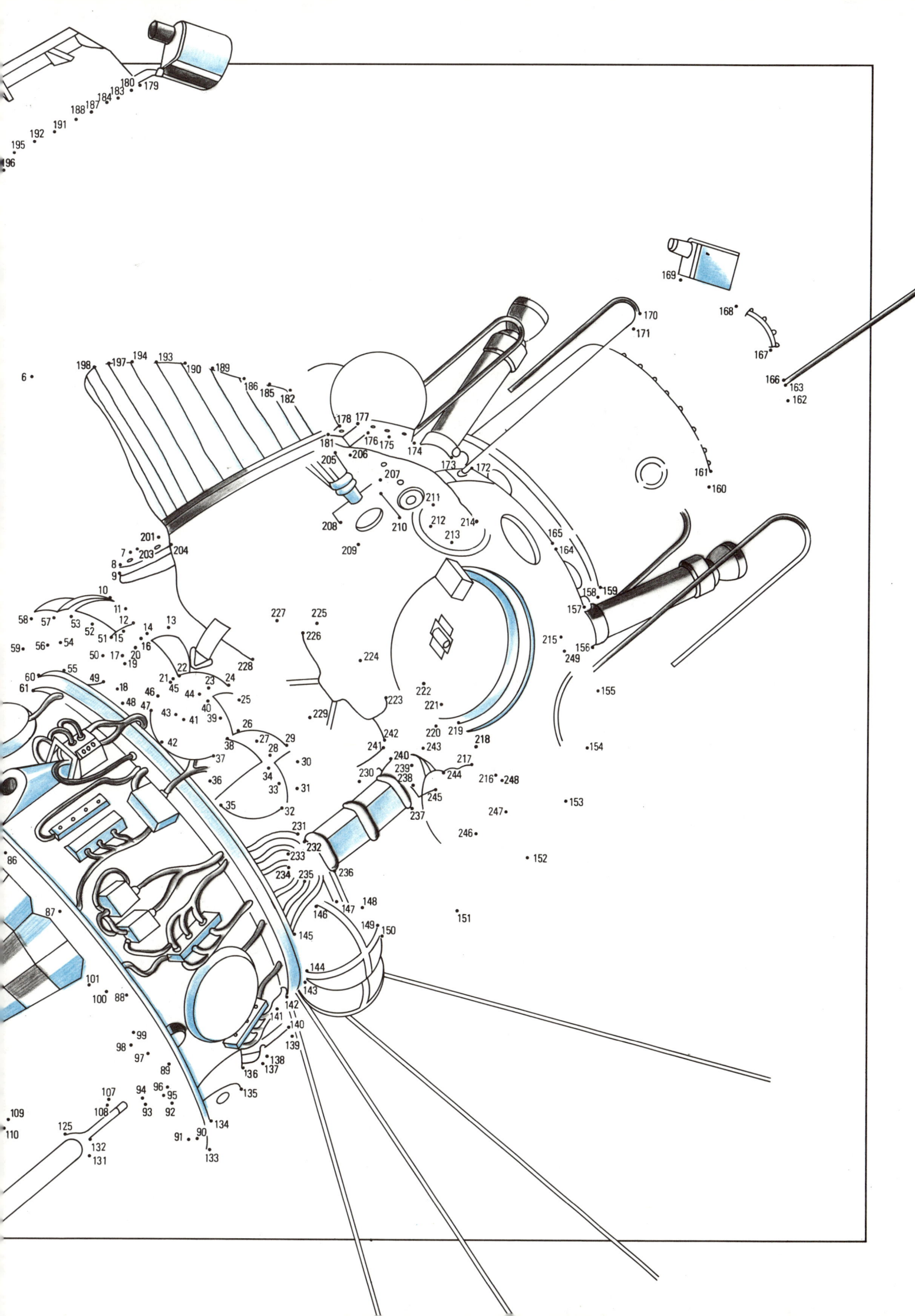

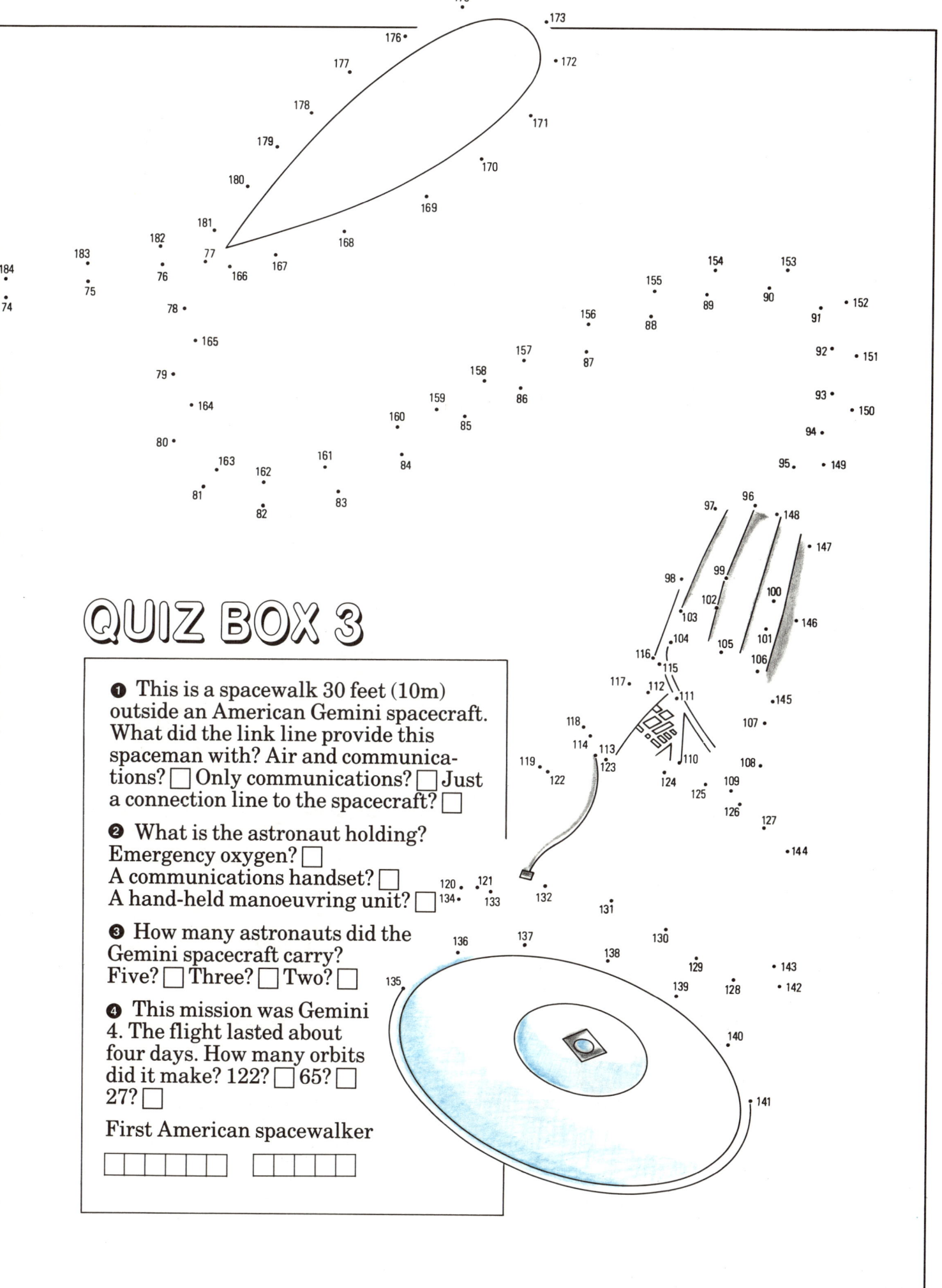

QUIZ BOX 3

❶ This is a spacewalk 30 feet (10m) outside an American Gemini spacecraft. What did the link line provide this spaceman with? Air and communications? ☐ Only communications? ☐ Just a connection line to the spacecraft? ☐

❷ What is the astronaut holding?
Emergency oxygen? ☐
A communications handset? ☐
A hand-held manoeuvring unit? ☐

❸ How many astronauts did the Gemini spacecraft carry?
Five? ☐ Three? ☐ Two? ☐

❹ This mission was Gemini 4. The flight lasted about four days. How many orbits did it make? 122? ☐ 65? ☐ 27? ☐

First American spacewalker

☐☐☐☐☐☐   ☐☐☐☐☐☐

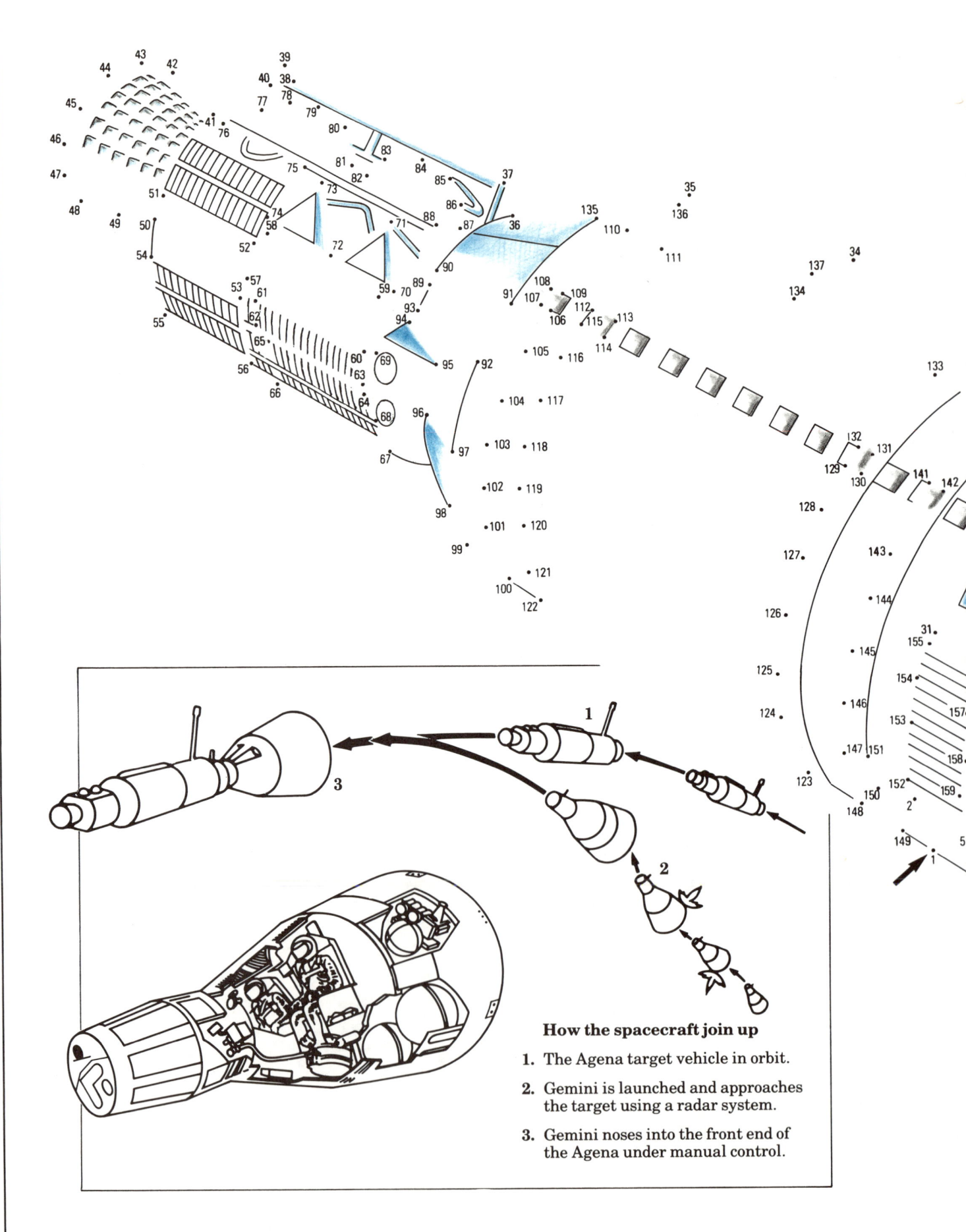

How the spacecraft join up

1. The Agena target vehicle in orbit.
2. Gemini is launched and approaches the target using a radar system.
3. Gemini noses into the front end of the Agena under manual control.

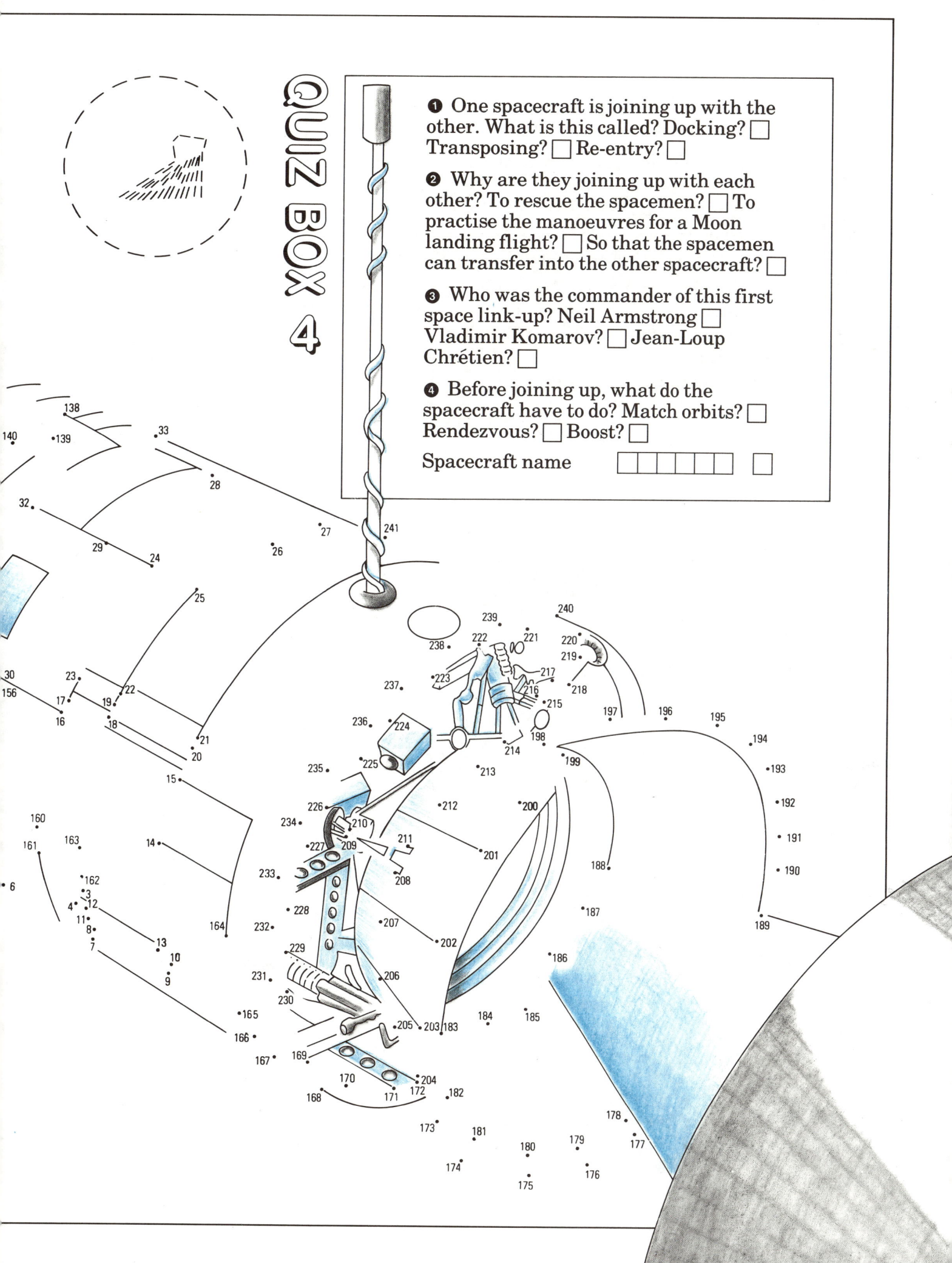

QUIZ BOX 5

❶ This is the first landing on the Moon. Which Apollo mission is it? Apollo 9? ☐ Apollo 11? ☐ Apollo 17? ☐

❷ What did the spacemen do on the Moon? Just walked around and took photos? ☐ Collected samples and laid out instruments? ☐ Planted a flag and then took off? ☐

❸ Where did the first men land on the Moon? The Ocean of Storms? ☐ The Sea of Tranquillity? ☐ Mare Crisium? ☐

❹ Neil Armstrong and Buzz Aldrin made footprints on the Moon. Did they disappear immediately? ☐ Are they still clearly visible? ☐ Have they been covered up by dust? ☐

Apollo landing craft name ☐☐☐☐☐

❶ How do you think this lunar buggy is powered? By batteries? ☐ By solar power? ☐ By small rockets? ☐

❷ What was its fastest speed on the Moon? 30 mph (48km/h)? ☐ 10 mph (16 km/h)? ☐ 2 mph (3km/h)? ☐

❸ How many American roving vehicles were driven on the Moon? Three? ☐ Four? ☐ Six? ☐

❹ The lunar buggy was equipped with a TV camera to give viewers on Earth a roving report. How was the camera operated? By the astronauts? ☐ Automatically? ☐ By an engineer on the Earth? ☐

Vehicle name ☐☐☐☐☐ ☐☐☐☐☐

QUIZ BOX 6

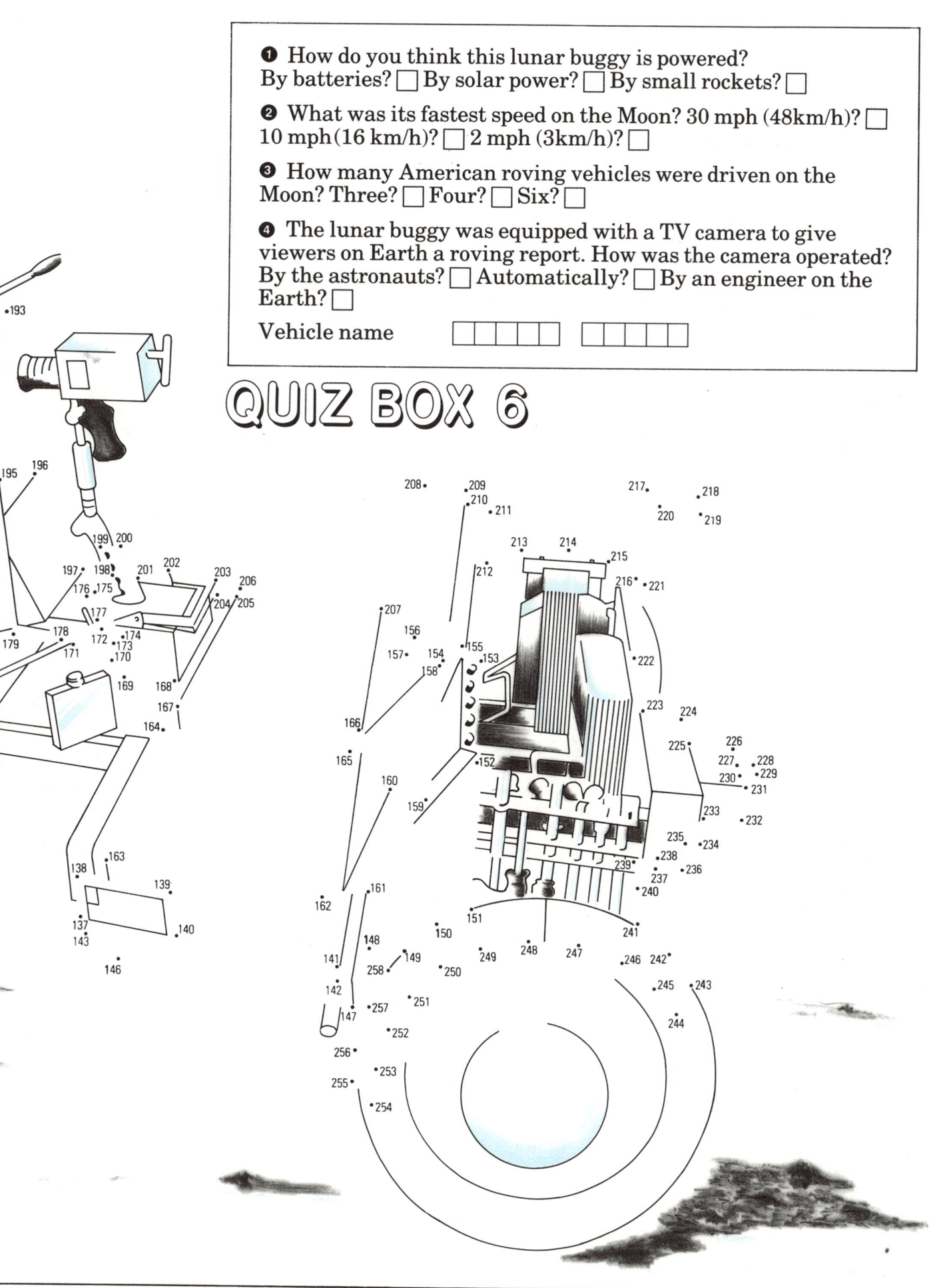

❶ Why did the Apollo spacecraft come down in the sea? Because the weather conditions were better? ☐ Because it was designed only to land at sea? ☐ It was off course and ended up in the sea? ☐

❷ At what speed did the three parachutes allow the spacecraft to hit the water? 30 mph (48 km/h)? ☐ 19 mph (30 km/h)? ☐ 10 mph (16 km/h)? ☐

❸ How many crew were inside the Apollo spacecraft when it landed? Two? ☐ Four? ☐ Three? ☐

❹ When Apollo landed, divers came to the rescue with rafts. What were the divers called? The recovery crew? ☐ The carrier crew? ☐ The ground team? ☐

Mission end ☐☐☐☐☐☐☐☐

QUIZ BOX 7

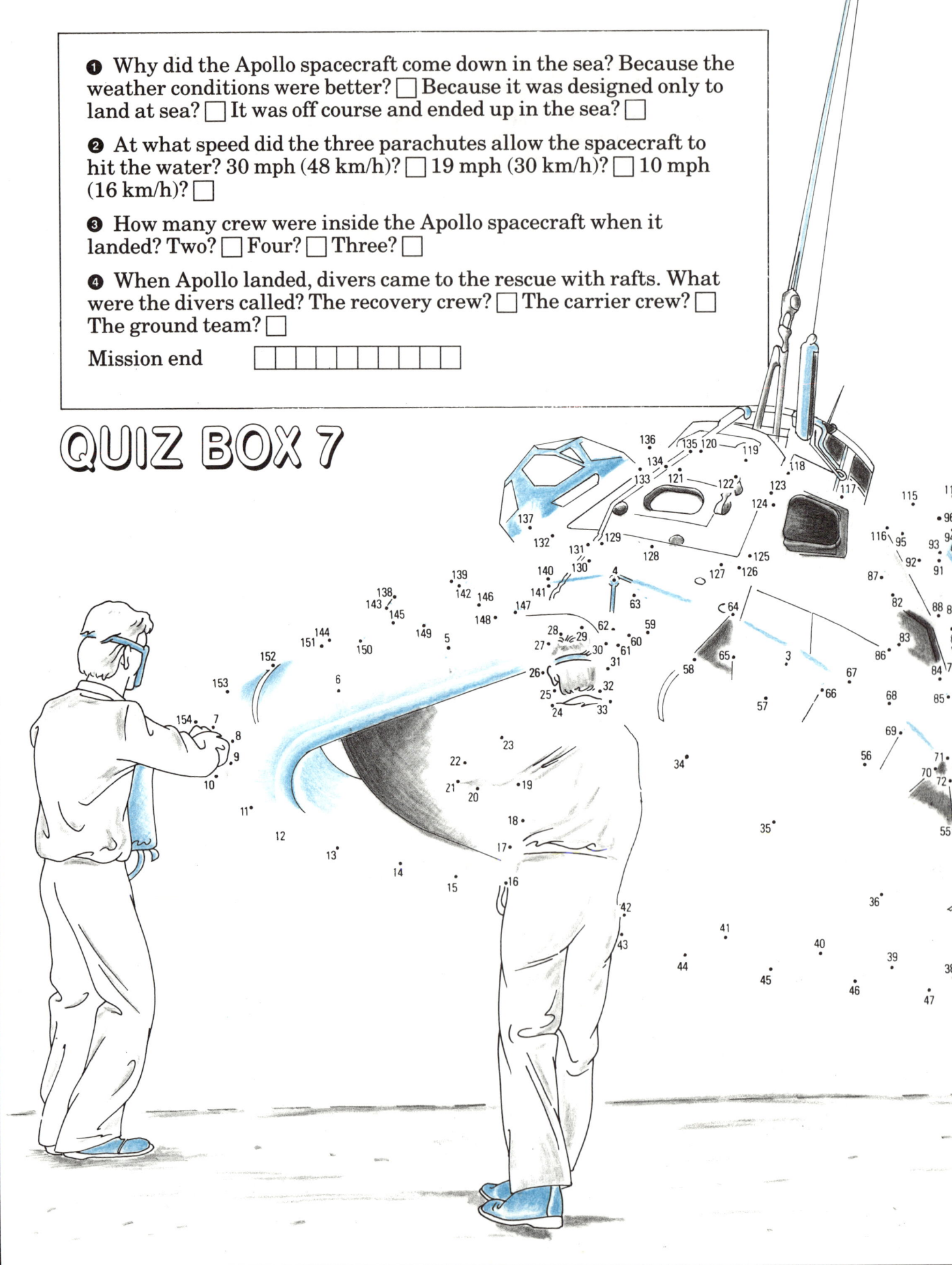

❶ Russian and American spacecraft docked in space for the first time in 1975. When did this next happen? In 1981? ☐ Never? ☐ In 1987? ☐

❷ How many men were in space together when the two spacecraft docked? Four? ☐ Six? ☐ Five? ☐

❸ Where did the Russians launch from? Cape Canaveral? ☐ Houston? ☐ Baikonur? ☐

❹ How long did the two spacecraft remain docked together? 7 hours? ☐ 43 hours? ☐ 72 hours? ☐

Mission name ☐☐☐☐☐☐ ☐☐☐☐☐

QUIZ BOX 8

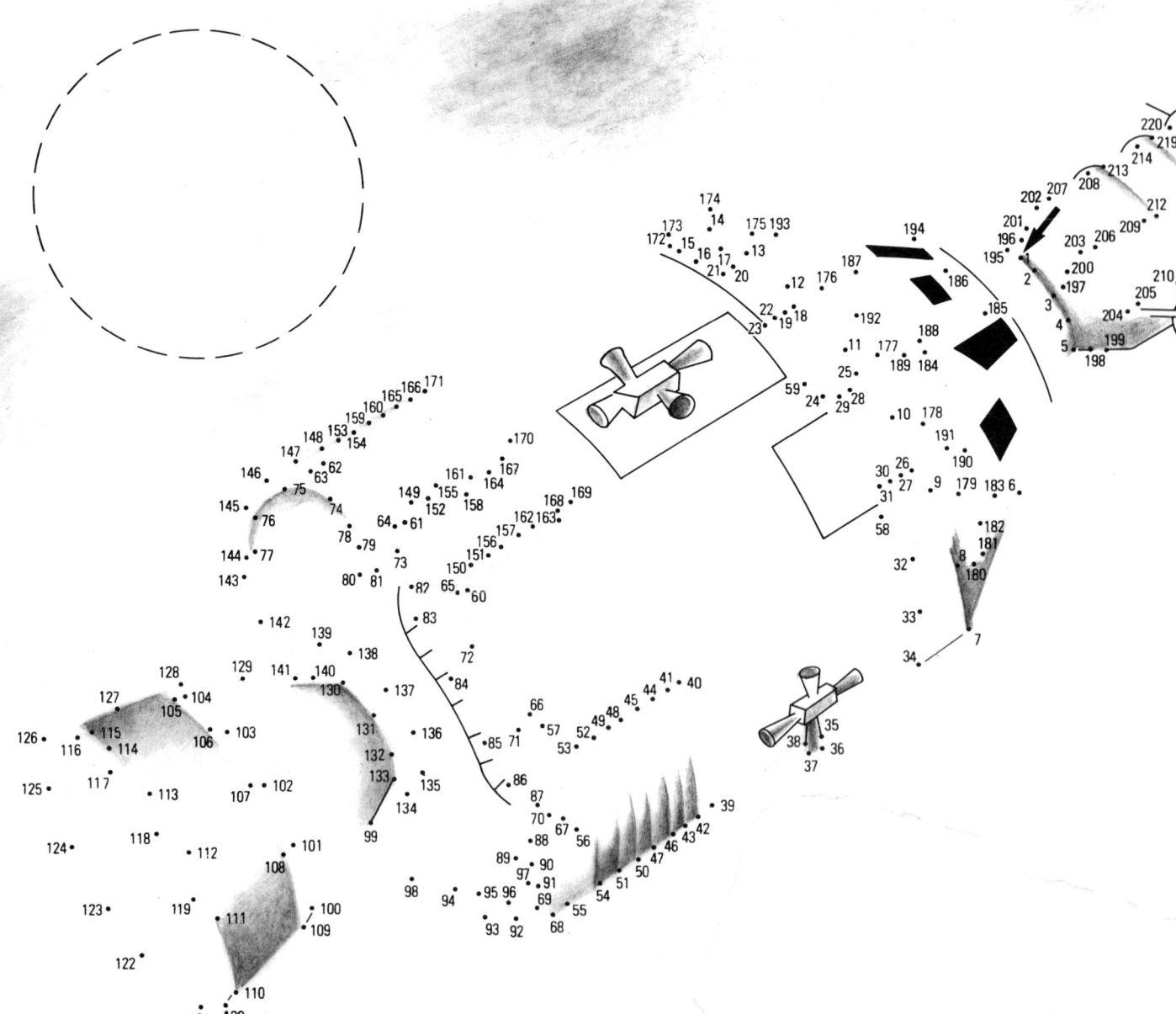

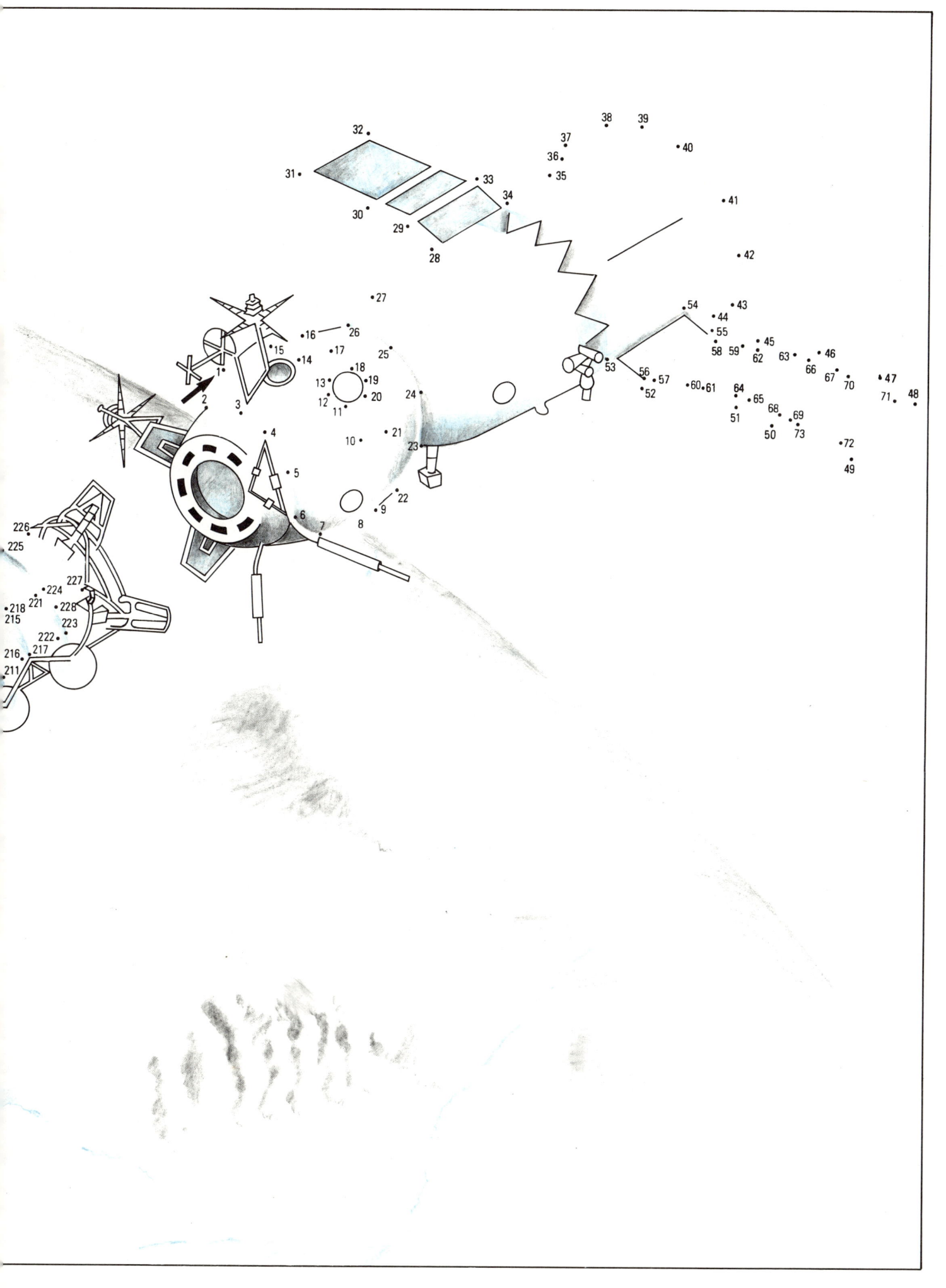

❶ This craft made the first soft landing, using parachute and retrorockets, onto the planet Mars in 1976. This year marked another celebration. What was it? International Spacefarers' Year? ☐ The 200th anniversary of the USA? ☐ 100 years after the birth of the science writer Jules Verne? ☐

❷ Mars has an atmosphere. What is the colour of the Martian sky, as first photographed by this spacecraft? Black? ☐ Pink? ☐ Blue? ☐

❸ This craft is the size of a small truck. What was the long metal pole used for? Scooping up the soil? ☐ Scanning for animal life? ☐ Measuring the heat of the surface? ☐

❹ How long did the spacecraft operate in the cold temperatures of Mars, with its hard frosts and sandstorms? 6 months? ☐ 1 year? ☐ 6 years? ☐

Spacecraft name ☐☐☐☐☐☐

QUIZ BOX 9

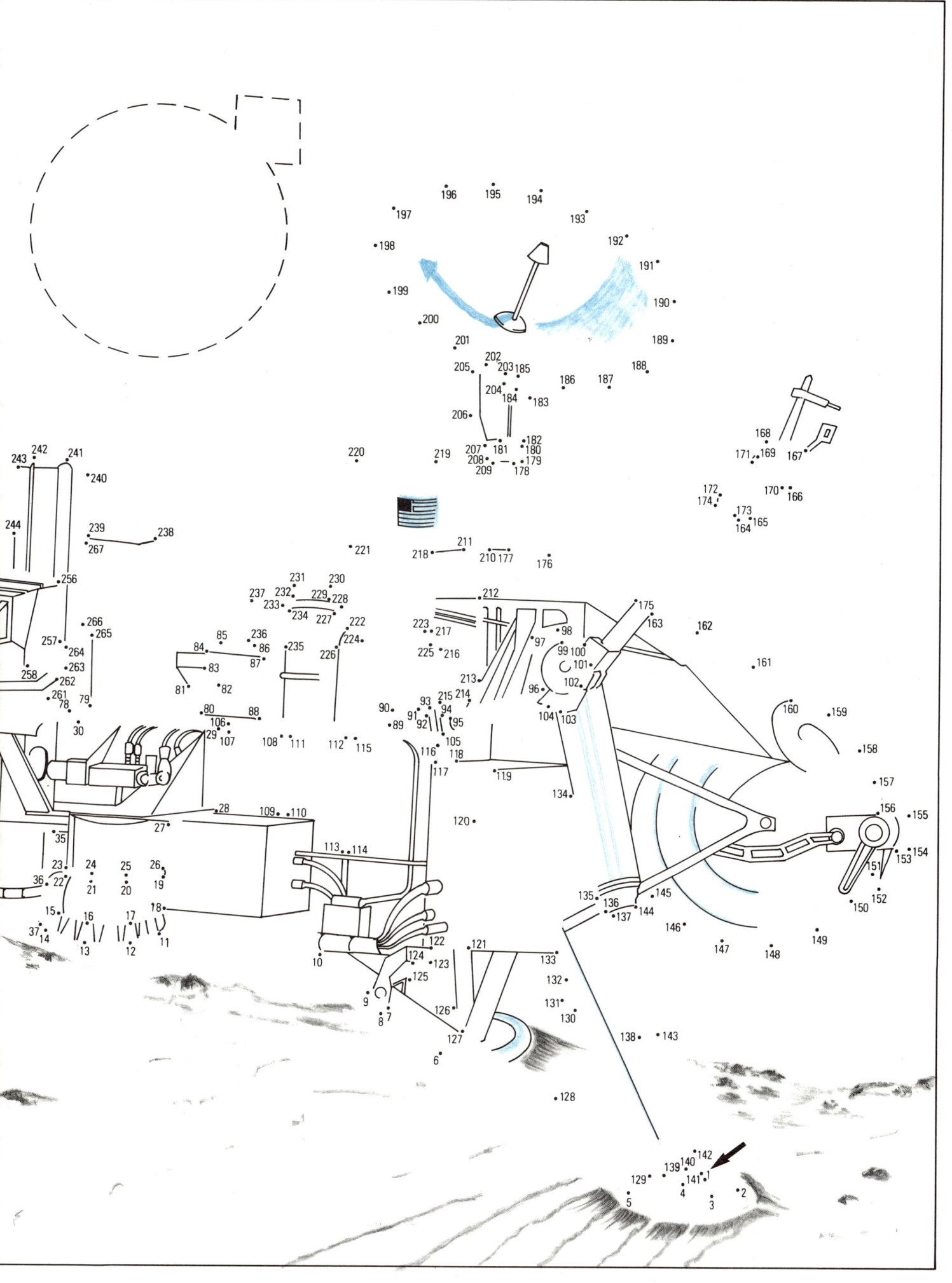

QUIZ BOX 10

❶ The first US Shuttle went through five tests in 1977. It was taken high up into the atmosphere and set free to glide back to Earth. The tests were called ALT. What does this stand for? Advanced Learning Tests? ☐ Approach and Landing Tests? ☐ Angle Line Timing? ☐

❷ The Shuttle is carried piggyback style on which adapted aircraft? Concorde? ☐ Jumbo? ☐ Tristar? ☐

❸ Where did the Shuttle tests take place? Cape Canaveral? ☐ White Sands Missile Base? ☐ Edwards Air Force Base? ☐

❹ The Shuttle was separated at about 5 miles (8 km) high. How long did it take to glide in to land? Under 10 minutes? ☐ Over 10 minutes? ☐ Over 20 minutes? ☐

Shuttle craft's name ☐☐☐☐☐☐☐☐☐

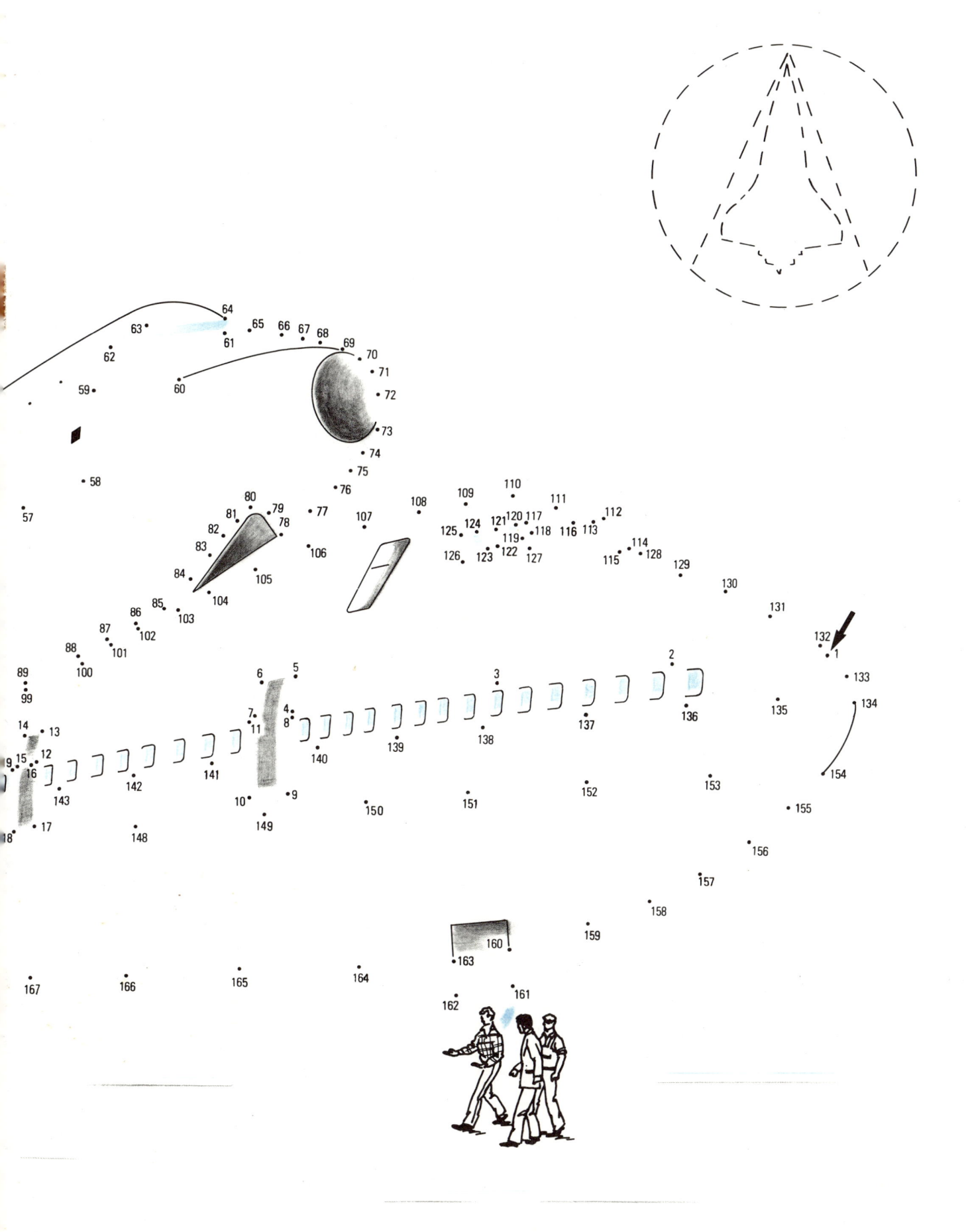

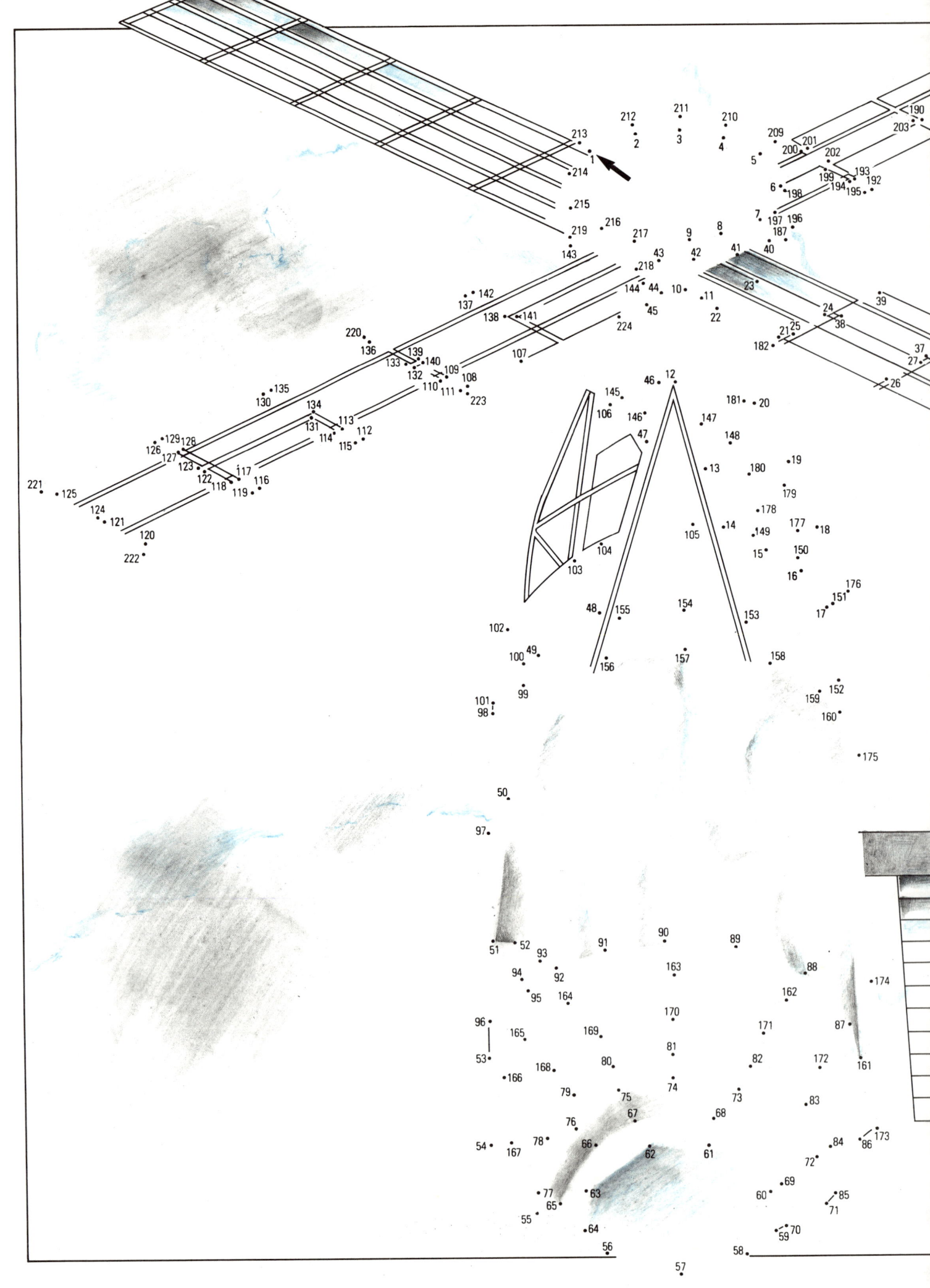

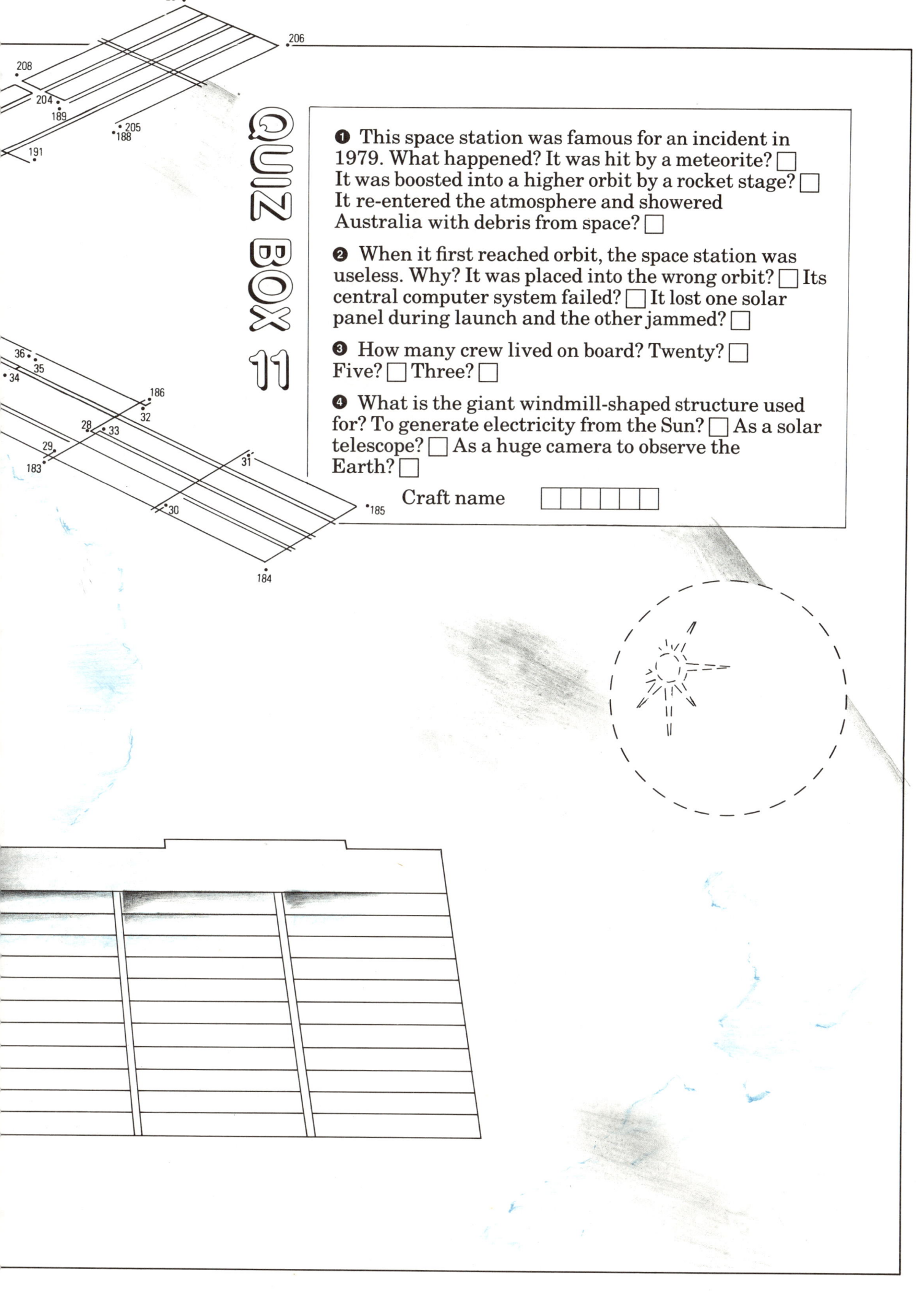

QUIZ BOX 11

❶ This space station was famous for an incident in 1979. What happened? It was hit by a meteorite? ☐ It was boosted into a higher orbit by a rocket stage? ☐ It re-entered the atmosphere and showered Australia with debris from space? ☐

❷ When it first reached orbit, the space station was useless. Why? It was placed into the wrong orbit? ☐ Its central computer system failed? ☐ It lost one solar panel during launch and the other jammed? ☐

❸ How many crew lived on board? Twenty? ☐ Five? ☐ Three? ☐

❹ What is the giant windmill-shaped structure used for? To generate electricity from the Sun? ☐ As a solar telescope? ☐ As a huge camera to observe the Earth? ☐

Craft name ☐☐☐☐☐☐

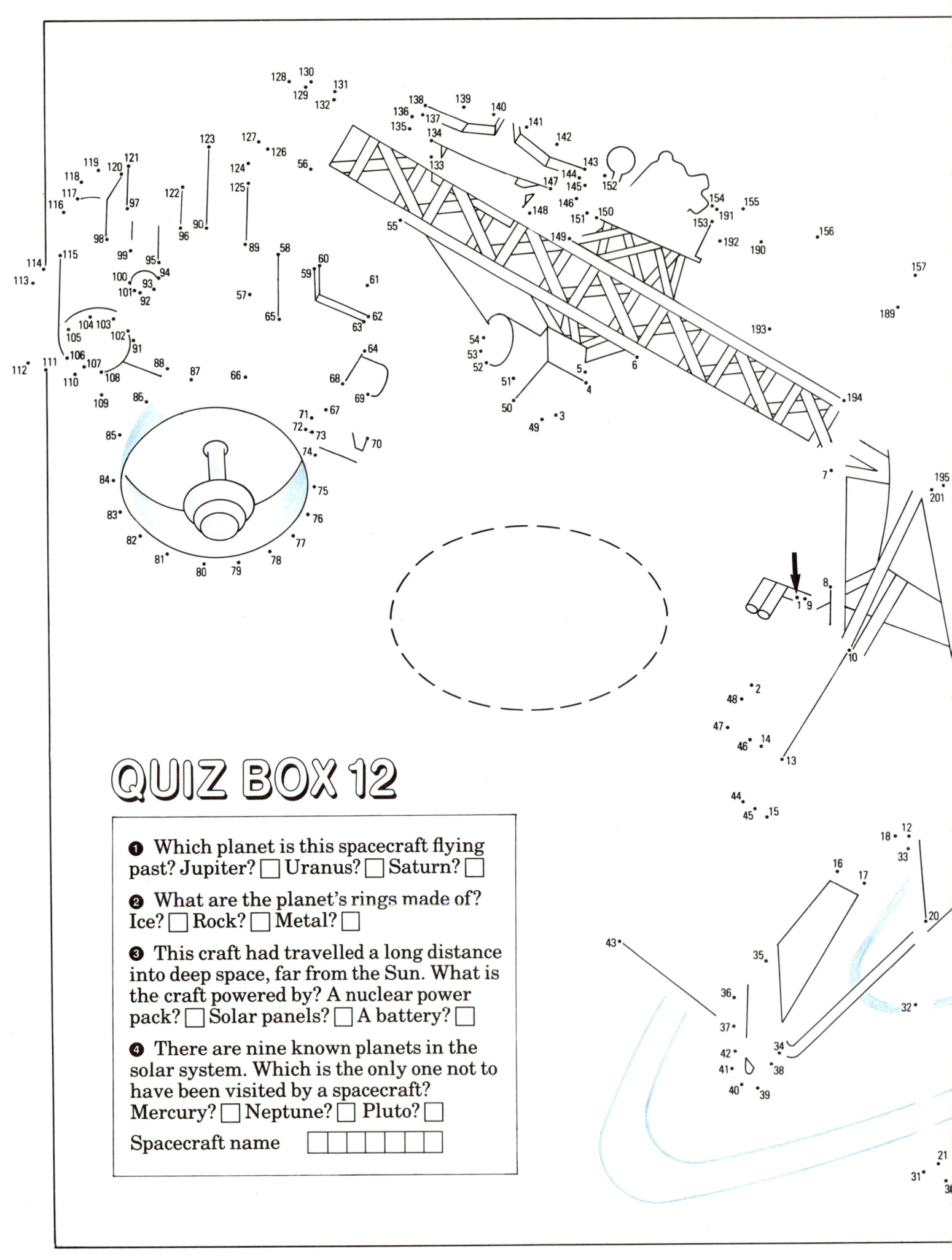

QUIZ BOX 12

❶ Which planet is this spacecraft flying past? Jupiter? ☐ Uranus? ☐ Saturn? ☐

❷ What are the planet's rings made of? Ice? ☐ Rock? ☐ Metal? ☐

❸ This craft had travelled a long distance into deep space, far from the Sun. What is the craft powered by? A nuclear power pack? ☐ Solar panels? ☐ A battery? ☐

❹ There are nine known planets in the solar system. Which is the only one not to have been visited by a spacecraft? Mercury? ☐ Neptune? ☐ Pluto? ☐

Spacecraft name ☐☐☐☐☐☐☐

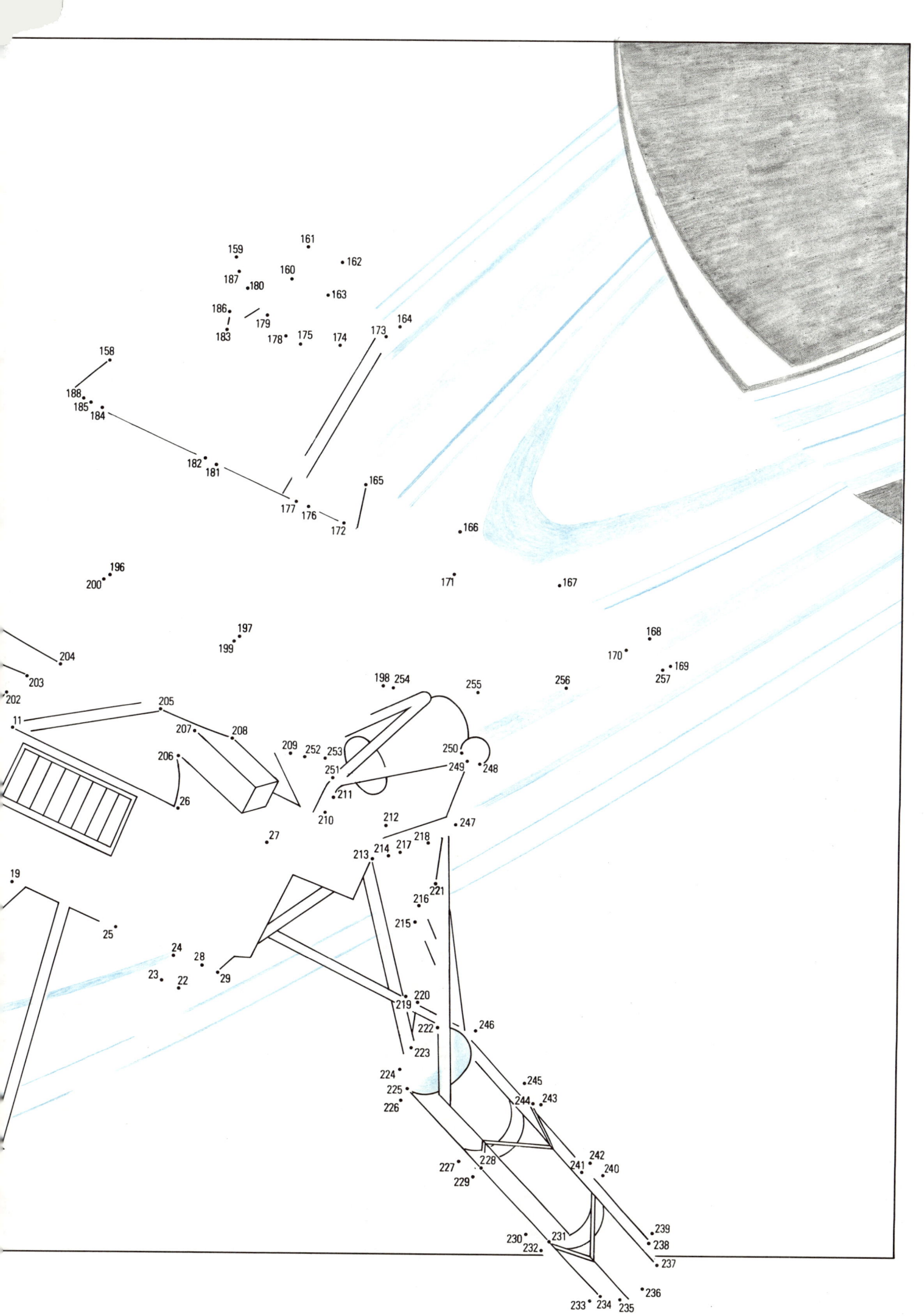

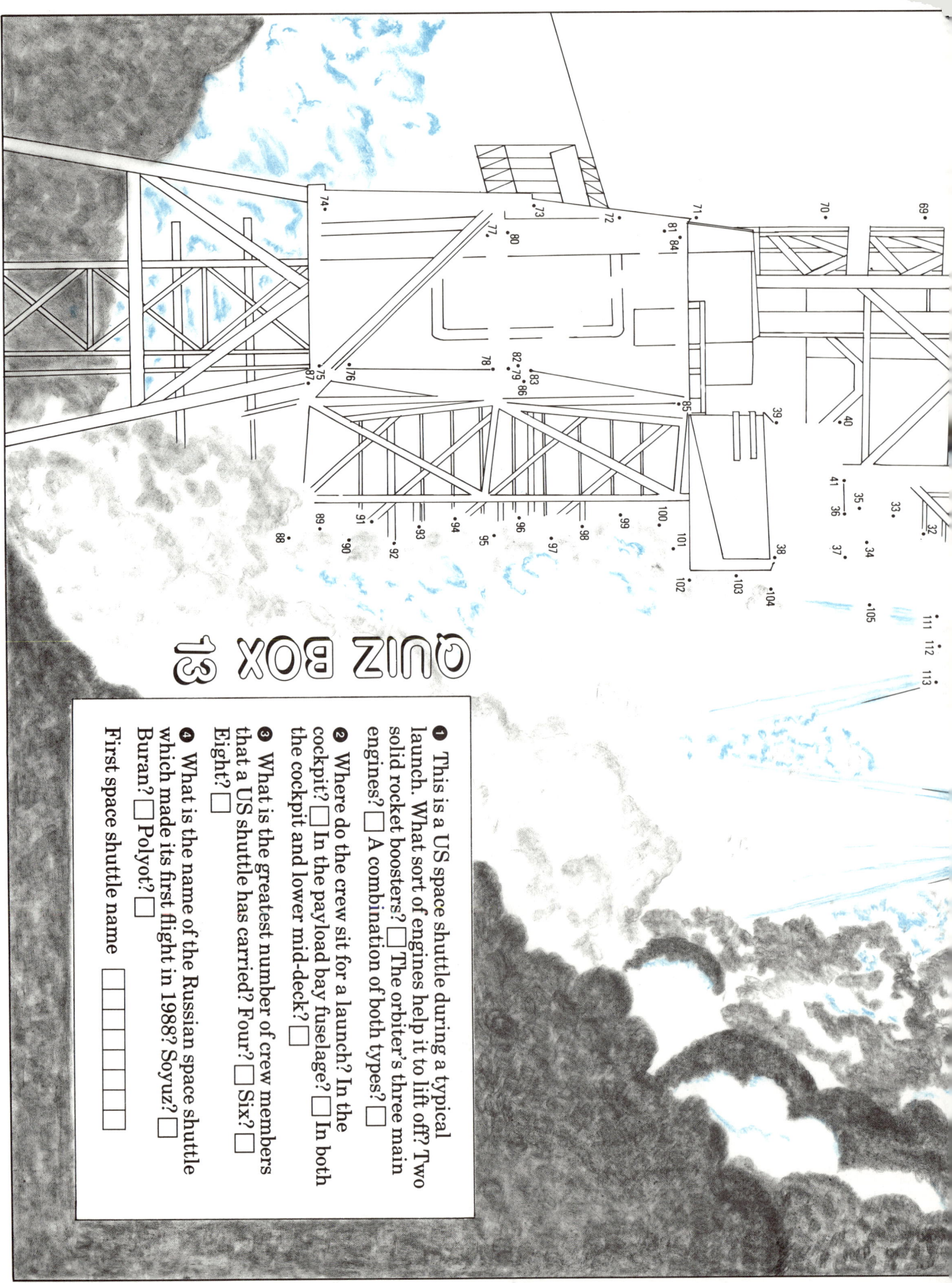

QUIZ BOX 13

❶ This is a US space shuttle during a typical launch. What sort of engines help it to lift off? Two solid rocket boosters? ☐ The orbiter's three main engines? ☐ A combination of both types? ☐

❷ Where do the crew sit for a launch? In the cockpit? ☐ In the payload bay fuselage? ☐ In both the cockpit and lower mid-deck? ☐

❸ What is the greatest number of crew members that a US shuttle has carried? Four? ☐ Six? ☐ Eight? ☐

❹ What is the name of the Russian space shuttle which made its first flight in 1988? Soyuz? ☐ Buran? ☐ Polyot? ☐

First space shuttle name ☐☐☐☐☐☐☐

❶ This spacecraft is as big as a furniture van, and it explored the planet Jupiter, about 486 million miles from the Sun. How long did it take to get to Jupiter? 4 months? ☐ 1 year 9 months? ☐ 2 years 6 months? ☐

❷ When it was sent towards Jupiter, the craft reached a record speed of 32,293 mph (51,969 km/h) or 21 times the speed of Concorde. How many hours had it been travelling when it went past the Moon? 5? ☐ 11? ☐ 31? ☐

❸ The craft took a picture of a huge round blob on Jupiter. What is the blob called? The Great Red Spot? ☐ The Hadley Rille? ☐ The Black Hole? ☐

❹ The spacecraft discovered that Jupiter has more than the 12 moons it was thought to have. How many moons does it have? 15? ☐ 21? ☐ 32? ☐

Spacecraft name ☐☐☐☐☐☐☐ ☐☐

QUIZ BOX 14

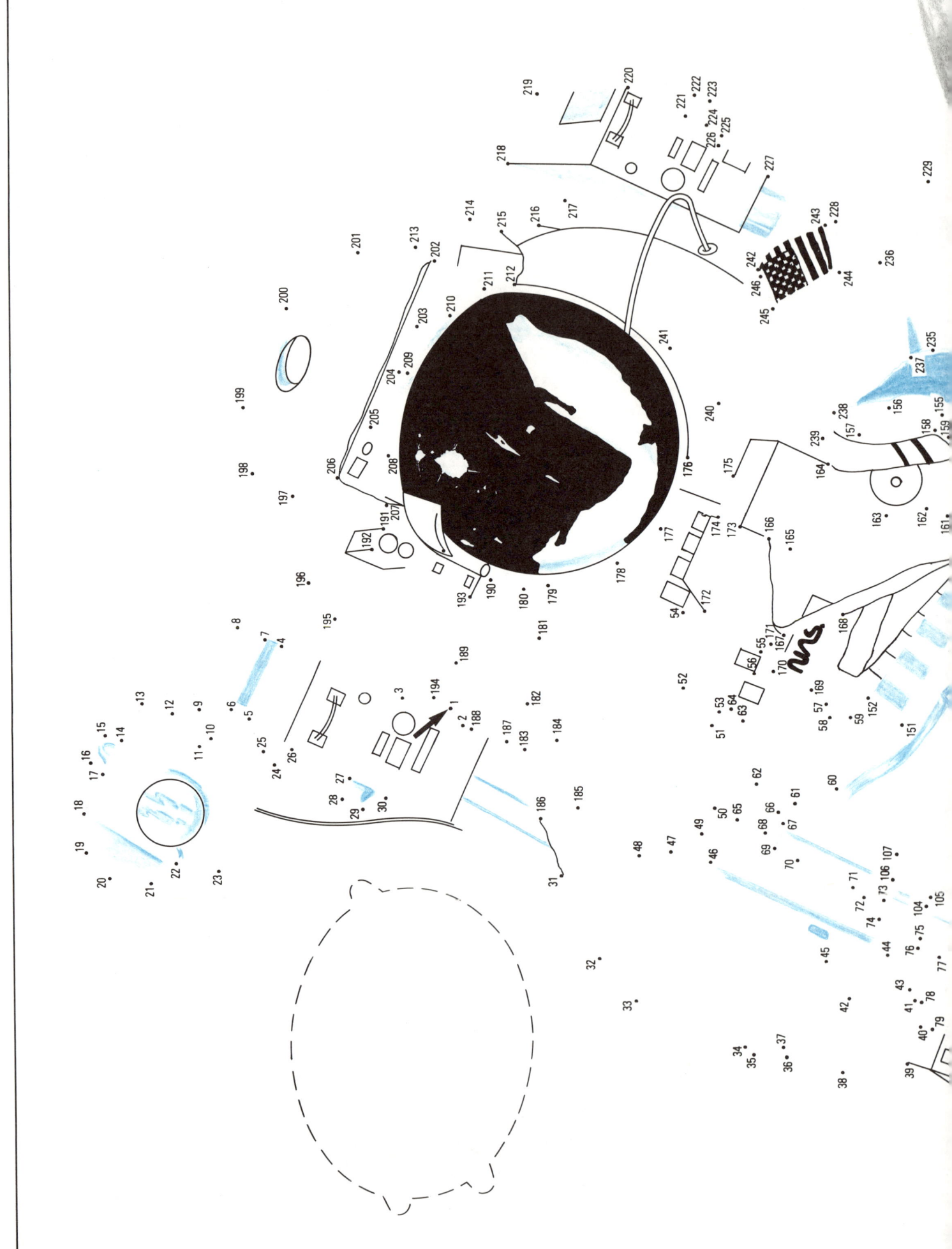

QUIZ BOX 16

❶ Svetlana Savitskaya is a female cosmonaut. What was she famous for doing aboard this space station? She made the first female spacewalk? ☐ She was the first to have a baby in space? ☐ She was the first to get married in space? ☐

❷ Who was the first woman to make two spaceflights? Sally Ride? ☐ Svetlana Savitskaya? ☐ Valentina Tereshkova? ☐

❸ This space station was launched in 1982. When was the first space station launched? 1971? ☐ 1973? ☐ 1978? ☐

❹ How long is this space station? As long as an airliner? ☐ A coach? ☐ A saloon car? ☐

Space station name ☐☐☐☐☐ ☐

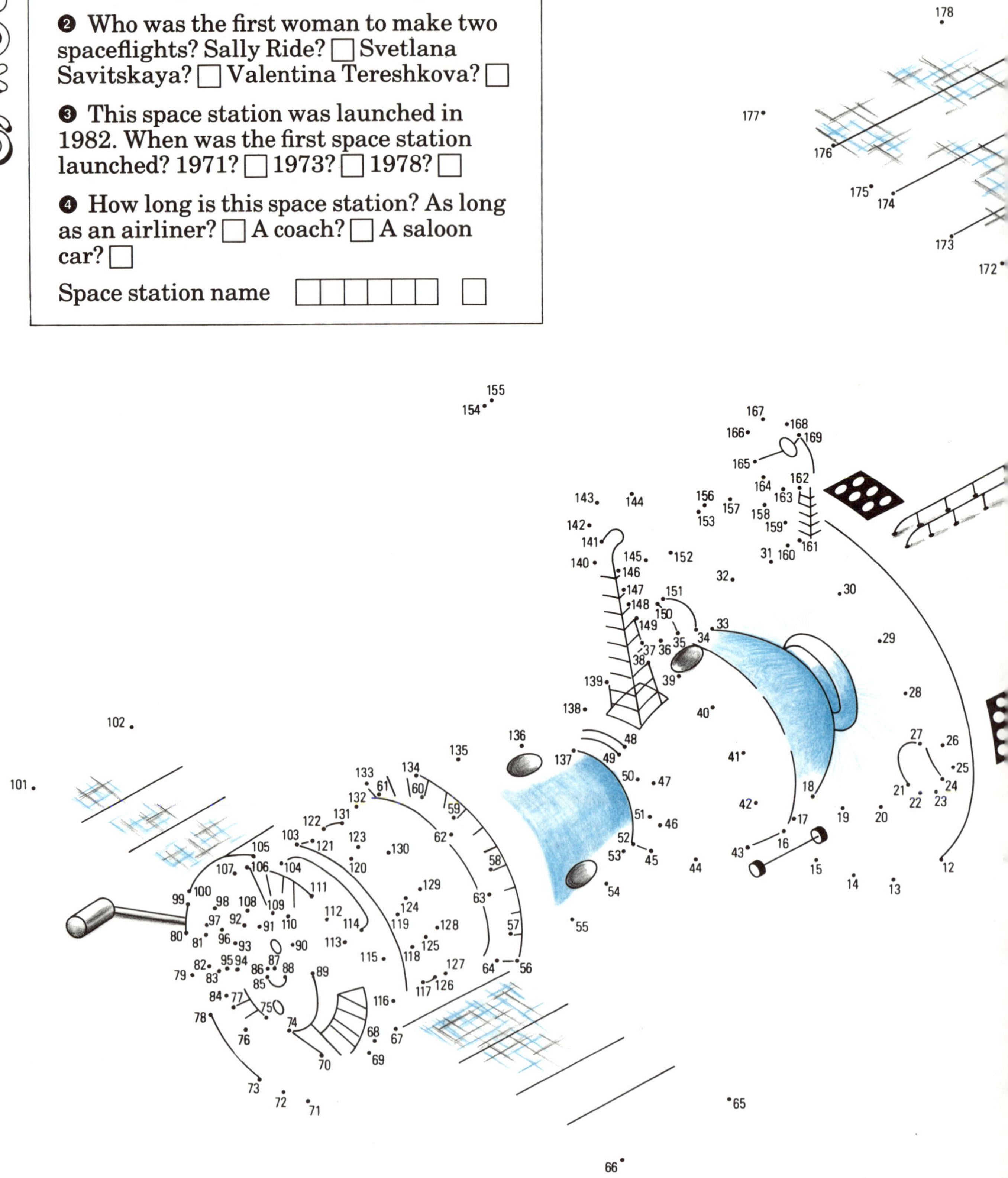

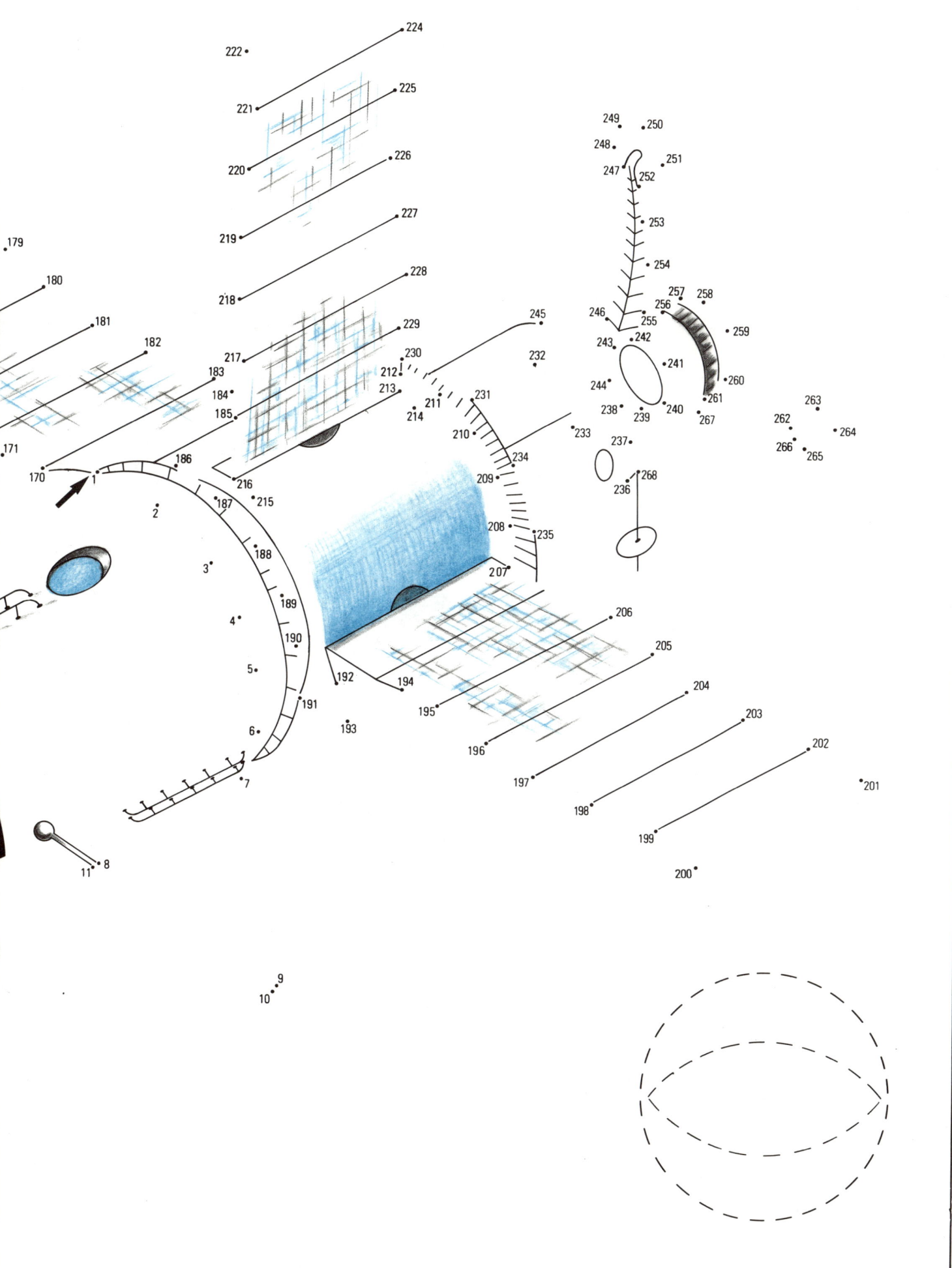

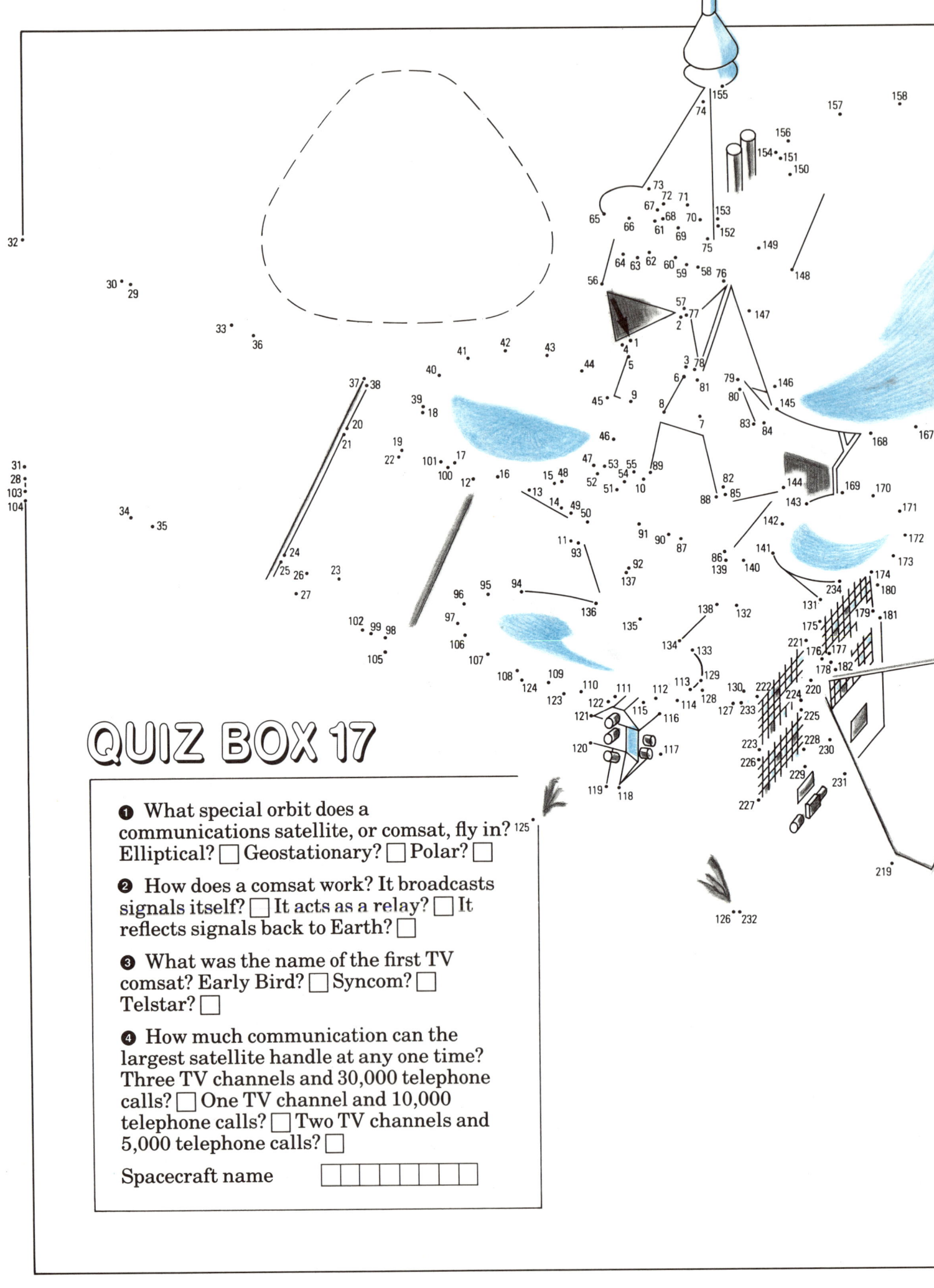

QUIZ BOX 17

❶ What special orbit does a communications satellite, or comsat, fly in? Elliptical? ☐ Geostationary? ☐ Polar? ☐

❷ How does a comsat work? It broadcasts signals itself? ☐ It acts as a relay? ☐ It reflects signals back to Earth? ☐

❸ What was the name of the first TV comsat? Early Bird? ☐ Syncom? ☐ Telstar? ☐

❹ How much communication can the largest satellite handle at any one time? Three TV channels and 30,000 telephone calls? ☐ One TV channel and 10,000 telephone calls? ☐ Two TV channels and 5,000 telephone calls? ☐

Spacecraft name ☐☐☐☐☐☐☐☐

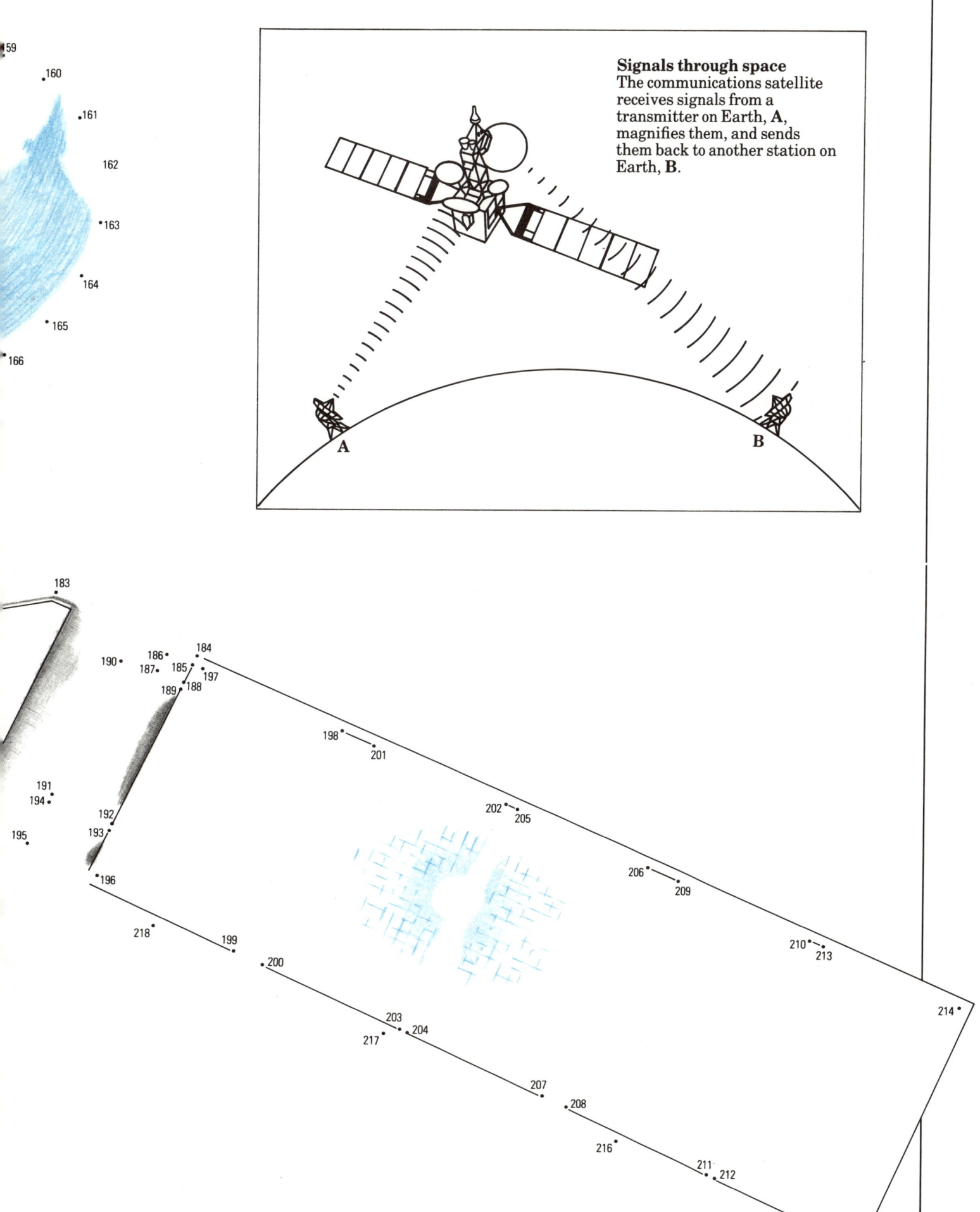

Signals through space
The communications satellite receives signals from a transmitter on Earth, **A**, magnifies them, and sends them back to another station on Earth, **B**.

QUIZ BOX 18

❶ This unmanned space probe, Giotto, was sent to explore a comet. How did it remain stable as it plunged through the comet? By using gas thrusters? ☐ By spinning like a top? ☐ By using the gravity force of the comet? ☐

❷ What did Giotto find inside the comet? A large rock? ☐ A big snowball? ☐ A ball of gas? ☐

❸ Who was Giotto named after? The person who discovered the comet? ☐ A famous astronomer? ☐ An Italian painter? ☐

❹ How often does this comet return? Every 10 years? ☐ 76 years? ☐ 105 years? ☐

Comet name

☐☐☐☐☐☐☐ ☐☐☐☐☐

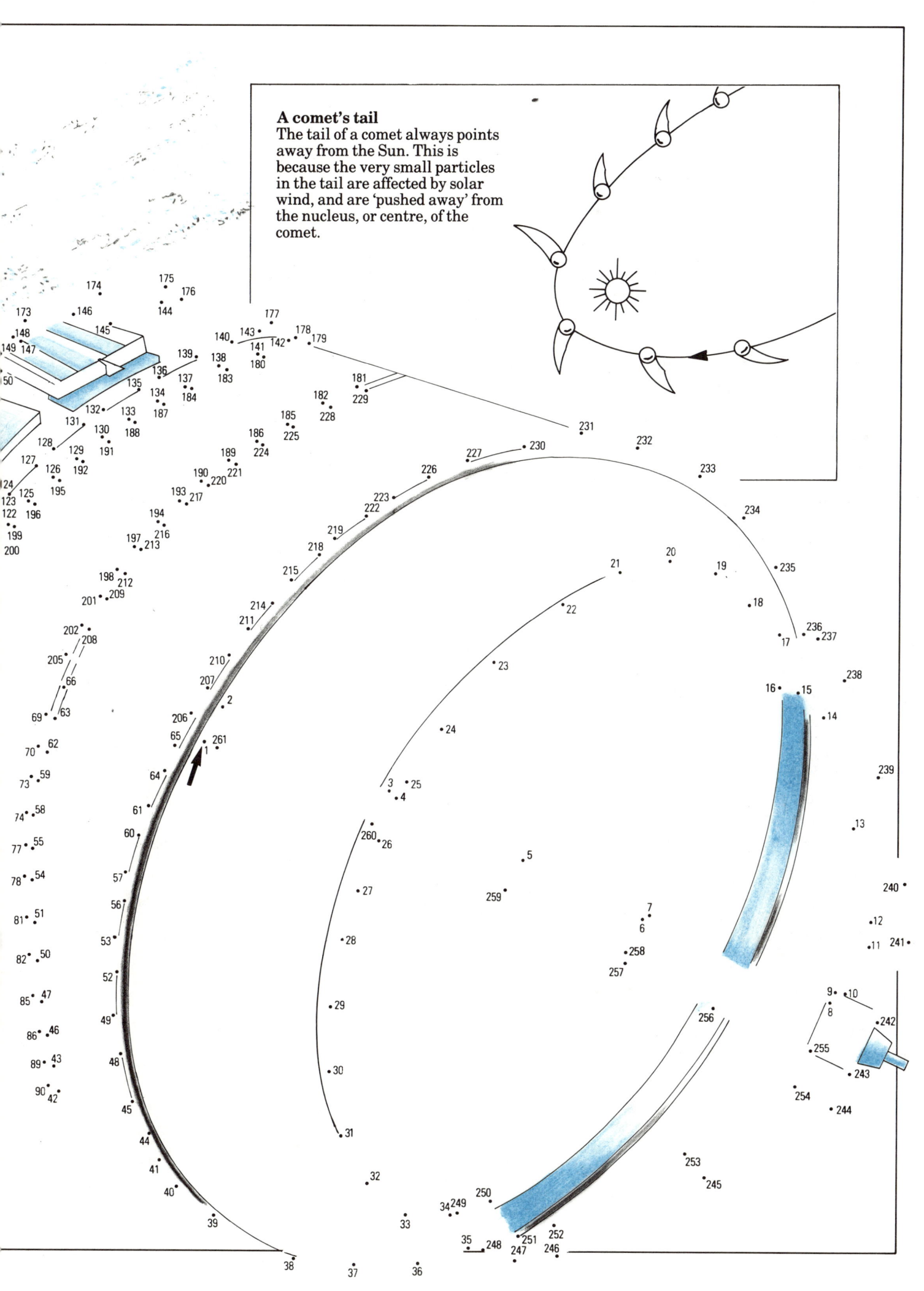

QUIZ BOX ANSWERS

PUZZLE 1

YURI GAGARIN

❶ Yuri Gagarin was **Russian**, which is why he was called a cosmonaut. Americans call their spacemen astronauts. A French spaceman is a spacionaute. 1 POINT

❷ The Vostok's landing onto the ground was too hard and Gagarin **would not have survived landing inside it.** 3 POINTS

❸ Gagarin entered an orbit nearly 200 miles (321 km) above the Earth. An orbit of this type takes about 90 minutes. The whole flight took **1 hour 48 minutes.** 3 POINTS

❹ In Russian, Vostok means **east.** The spacecraft was launched towards the east from Baikonur Cosmodrome. 2 POINTS

TOTAL SCORED ☐

PUZZLE 2

ALEXEI LEONOV

❶ A spacewalk is called **extravehicular activity**, or **EVA**. This term is more often used by the Americans. 1 POINT

❷ Leonov received oxygen from his back pack, rather like a diver. The link line was used for **communications**. He did not need water for such a short spacewalk. 2 POINTS

❸ Leonov spent about 20 minutes outside, although his spacewalk lasted only **12 minutes 9 seconds.** He found it very difficult to get back inside! 3 POINTS

❹ Voskhod was equipped with soft landing rockets. The spacecraft strayed off course and **landed in a forest** and the crew had to spend a night inside the capsule, hiding from hungry wolves! 2 POINTS

TOTAL SCORED ☐

THE FIRST ROCKETS

Here are four of the many rockets that have been used to launch men into space. The first was the Vostok, which launched Yuri Gagarin in 1961. The Voskhod was an improved version of the Vostok. Look at the size of the US Titan boosters and compare them with those of Saturn 5. The Titan was used to launch the Gemini spacecraft, weighing about 8,300 pounds (3,764 kg), into orbit around the Earth. The Saturn 5 had to be large enough to launch the 103,000 pound (46,720 kg) Apollo spacecraft to the Moon.

1. Vostok: 126 feet (38m)
2. Voskhod: 143 feet (44m)
3. Titan II: 109 feet (33m)
4. Saturn 5: 363 feet (111m)

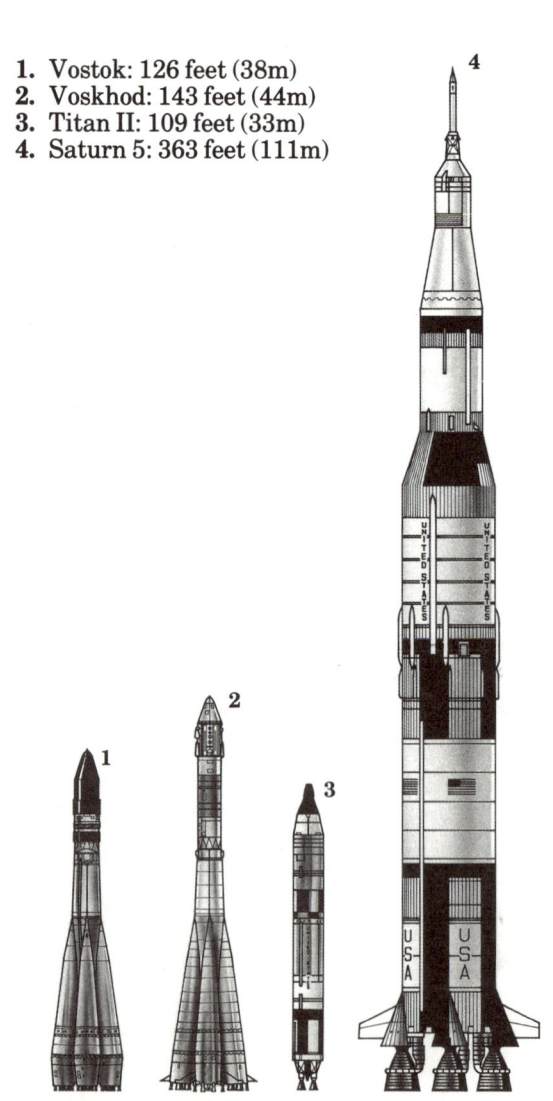

How did you score?

PUZZLE 3

EDWARD WHITE

❶ White's link line carried both **air and a communications wire**. 3 POINTS

❷ White is holding a **hand-held manoeuvring unit**. This helped him to move around and still keep in a stable position while he was weightless in space. 1 POINT

❸ Gemini was named after the constellation of stars called the Heavenly Twins because it carried **two crew**. 1 POINT

❹ It takes about 90 minutes to make one orbit. The Gemini 4 flight made **65 orbits**. 3 POINTS

TOTAL SCORED ☐

PUZZLE 4

GEMINI 8

❶ The two spacecraft joining up in space are **docking** with each other. This is a very complicated manoeuvre and was one of the triumphs of the Space Age. 1 POINT

❷ The Gemini dockings were used **to practise manoeuvres for later Moon landings** when the landing craft would take off from the Moon to meet up with its mother ship in orbit around the Moon. 2 POINTS

❸ **Neil Armstrong**. He wasn't just the first man on the Moon, he was the first to dock in space, too. 3 POINTS

❹ Before docking, the active spacecraft, Gemini, has a lot of manoeuvring to do before it meets up with the target. This is called **rendezvous**. 2 POINTS

TOTAL SCORED ☐

PUZZLE 5

EAGLE

❶ The first landing on the Moon was made by **Apollo 11**. 2 POINTS

❷ The astronauts spent a rushed 2 hours 40 minutes **collecting samples and laying out instruments**. 2 POINTS. They also erected a flag (but no points for this).

❸ Armstrong and Aldrin landed in the **Sea of Tranquillity**. The first words from the Moon were, "Tranquillity Base here, the Eagle has landed." 2 POINTS

❹ There is no atmosphere on the Moon, so the footprints lie undisturbed and **are still clearly visible** after 20 years. 3 POINTS

TOTAL SCORED ☐

PUZZLE 6

LUNAR ROVER

❶ The Lunar Rover was powered by a **battery**. It arrived on the Moon folded and packed into the side of the lunar module. It was taken out and unfolded by the astronauts on the Moon. 2 POINTS

❷ The fastest speed achieved by a Lunar Rover on the Moon was **10 mph (16 km/h)**. John Young, the commander of Apollo 16, was the driver. 3 POINTS

❸ **Three** Lunar Rovers were driven on the Moon. The first Lunar Rover was driven during the Apollo 15 mission. The Russians put two Lunokhods on the Moon and operated them from Earth. 2 POINTS

❹ The camera on the Lunar Rover was operated **by an engineer on Earth!** 3 POINTS

TOTAL SCORED ☐

QUIZ BOX ANSWERS

EXPLORING THE PLANETS

Venus was explored for the first time in 1962 by the American craft, Mariner 2. Mariner 4 took the first pictures of Mars in 1985. A Russian probe has sent back pictures from the surface of Venus. Mercury was explored by Mariner 10. Jupiter has been explored four times, Saturn three times, and Uranus and Neptune once. There are no plans at the moment to explore Pluto. It would take ten years to get there.

Figures refer to distance in millions from the Sun.

Pluto 3,666 mi/5,898 km
Neptune 2,793 mi/4,493 km
Uranus 1,783 mi/2,870 km
Saturn 886 mi/1,426 km
Jupiter 483 mi/779 km
Mars 141.5 mi/228 km
Earth 93 mi/150 km — Moon
Venus 67 mi/108 km
Mercury 36 mi/58 km

PUZZLE 7

SPLASHDOWN

❶ Apollo was **designed to land safely at sea**. If it strayed off course, however, it could land on the ground in an emergency, but the crew would not have been very comfortable. 2 POINTS

❷ The speed of landing was **19 mph (30 km/h)**. All the astronauts felt was a hard jolt. 3 POINTS

❸ Apollo had a crew of **three**. It was used as a stand-by emergency rescue vehicle for the Skylab programme, and could be equipped to carry five crew members. 2 POINTS

❹ The divers were called the **recovery crew**. 1 POINT

TOTAL SCORED

PUZZLE 8

APOLLO-SOYUZ

❶ There has **never** been another joint flight between the two nations and many people say this is a pity. It is possible that the USA and USSR will cooperate on a future mission to land men on the planet Mars. 2 POINTS

❷ There were three Americans and two Russians in space, making a total of **five**. The Americans were Tom Stafford, Vance Brand and Donald Slayton. The Russians were Alexei Leonov, the spacewalker, and Valeri Kubasov. 3 POINTS

❸ The Russians were launched from the **Baikonur Cosmodrome** in Kazakhstan. 2 POINTS

❹ Apollo and Soyuz remained docked together for **43 hours**. 2 POINTS

TOTAL SCORED

How did you score?

PUZZLE 9

VIKING

❶ 1976 was also the **200th anniversary of the USA**. Scientists had hoped that they could land Viking on the actual day of the anniversary, 4th July, but were delayed to 20th July. 3 POINTS

❷ The sky on Mars is **pink**. 1 POINT

❸ The pole had a **scoop to pick up the soil**. It was also used to dig a trench in the soil. The soil was poured into an instrument on the spacecraft and tested but no traces of life were found. 2 POINTS

❹ The amazing spacecraft finally broke down in 1982 — **6 years** after landing. 3 POINTS

TOTAL SCORED ☐

PUZZLE 11

SKYLAB

❶ Skylab **re-entered the Earth's atmosphere in 1979 and showered parts of Western Australia with pieces of debris**. 2 POINTS

❷ During launch, **one solar panel was torn away and the other jammed**. Astronauts made a brave spacewalk to free the jammed panel and saved the whole programme. 3 POINTS

❸ There were **three** crew members on Skylab. 1 POINT

❹ The windmill shaped structure is the **solar telescope**. Skylab helped scientists learn much more about the Sun. 3 POINTS

TOTAL SCORED ☐

PUZZLE 10

ENTERPRISE

❶ The tests were called **Approach and Landing Tests** (ALT). 2 POINTS

❷ The Shuttle rode piggyback on a modified **Jumbo** jet. 1 POINT

❸ The ALT tests were made from the NASA Dryden Research Centre at **Edwards Air Force Base**, California. White Sands Missile Base was used for the landing of the third Space Shuttle space mission in 1982. Cape Canaveral is the main launching site in the USA, although the Space Shuttle is actually launched from the Kennedy Space Centre, north of Cape Canaveral. 3 POINTS

❹ It took Enterprise **less than 10 minutes** to land after separation from the Jumbo Jet. 2 POINTS

TOTAL SCORED ☐

PUZZLE 12

VOYAGER

❶ The spacecraft is flying past the ringed planet **Saturn**. It was launched on 5th September, 1977 but did not reach Saturn until 12th November, 1980. 2 POINTS

❷ The rings turned out to be thousands of tiny ringlets of small particles of **ice**. 3 POINTS

❸ Batteries are no good since they would go flat during the long journey. The Sun is too far away for solar panels to work so the craft was powered by a **nuclear power pack**. 3 POINTS

❹ Spacecraft have visited all the known planets in the solar system except **Pluto** which is the furthest from Earth. Neptune is to be explored in August 1989 by Voyager 2. 1 POINT

TOTAL SCORED ☐

QUIZ BOX ANSWERS

THE SPACE SHUTTLE

The US Space Shuttle was first used simply to launch all the American satellites into orbit. Nowadays the Shuttle is used increasingly to perform tasks that it was especially designed to do, such as placing large structures in space, like this Space Telescope, *below*, and taking astronauts into space to repair satellites or assist in building space stations.

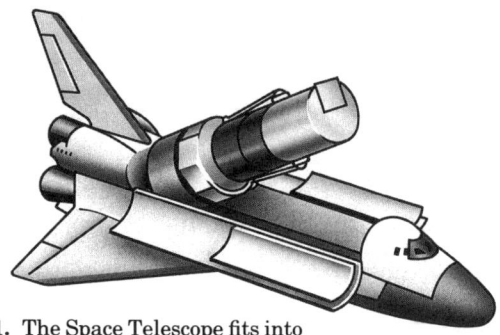

1. The Space Telescope fits into the shuttle orbiter.

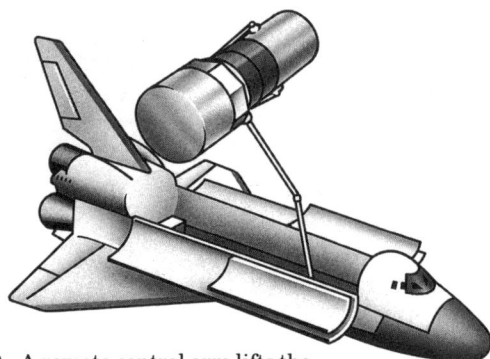

2. A remote control arm lifts the Telescope out.

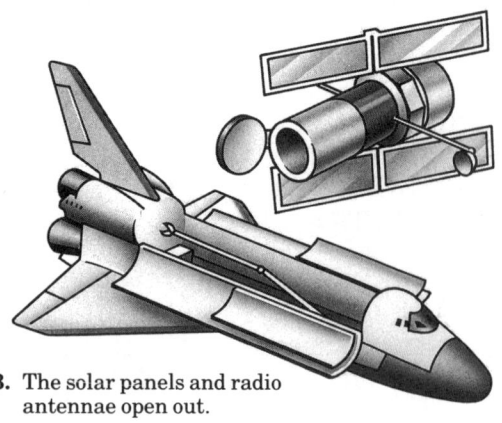

3. The solar panels and radio antennae open out.

PUZZLE 13

COLUMBIA

❶ Columbia is powered for launch with **a combination of the two solid rocket boosters and the orbiter's three main engines.** 1 POINT

❷ The commander, pilot and two mission specialists are seated **in the cockpit** for launch **and** the other crew members in **the lower mid-deck**. 3 POINTS

❸ The record number of people carried into space by one craft was **eight** on the 22nd Space Shuttle mission. 2 POINTS

❹ The Russian space shuttle is called **Buran**. On its first flight in 1988, it was unmanned. 2 POINTS

TOTAL SCORED

PUZZLE 14

PIONEER 10

❶ Pioneer 10 was launched on 3rd March, 1972 and reached Jupiter on 5th December, 1973, a journey of **1 year 9 months**. In 1983 it became the first spacecraft to leave the solar system. It could reach a new solar system about once every million years! 3 POINTS

❷ Pioneer 10 had been travelling for just **11 hours**. 2 POINTS

❸ The giant blob is called the **Great Red Spot** and can be seen from Earth with a telescope. It is a huge storm in the atmosphere of Jupiter and it is larger than the Earth. 2 POINTS

❹ Jupiter has **15 known moons** – and also a small ring system like Saturn. 3 POINTS

TOTAL SCORED

How did you score?

PUZZLE 15

BRUCE McCANDLESS

❶ MMU stands for **Manned Manoeuvring Unit**. 2 POINTS

❷ The MMU's gas is **nitrogen**. The Russian MMU will be powered by compressed air. 3 POINTS

❸ The MMU could move about **in all directions**, up and down, side to side, forwards and backwards. 2 POINTS

❹ Bruce McCandless was the first of **six Americans** to fly an MMU. The others are Robert Stewart – during the same mission as McCandless – Pinky Nelson and James van Hoften and Joe Allen and Dale Gardner. 3 POINTS

TOTAL SCORED ☐

PUZZLE 17

INTELSAT

❶ It travels in a **geostationary orbit**. This means that the satellite travels around the Earth's equator in an orbit, at a constant height and speed so that it is always above the same location. 2 POINTS

❷ The communications satellite receives signals, amplifies them, and sends them back, so it is a **relay** satellite. 3 POINTS

❸ **Telstar** was the first communications satellite, set up in 1962. 1 POINT

❹ Intelsat VI is the size of a big living room and can handle **three TV channels and 30,000 telephone calls** at once. 2 POINTS

TOTAL SCORED ☐

PUZZLE 16

SALYUT 7

❶ Svetlana Savitskaya was the **first woman to make a spacewalk,** from the Russian Salyut 7 space station in 1984. The first American woman to spacewalk was Kathy Sullivan, also in 1984. 2 POINTS

❷ **Savitskaya** was also the first woman to make two spaceflights. The first American woman to do this was Sally Ride, again in 1984. Valentina Tereshkova was the first woman ever to make a spaceflight, in Vostok 6, in 1963. 3 POINTS

❸ The first Salyut space station was launched in **1971**. The first American space station, Skylab, was launched two years later. 3 POINTS

❹ Salyut 7 was as long as a tourist **coach**. 2 POINTS

TOTAL SCORED ☐

PUZZLE 18

HALLEY'S COMET

❶ The Giotto probe was as tall as a man and remained stable **by spinning like a top**. 2 POINTS

❷ The inside, or nucleus, of Halley's Comet is a potato-shaped **rock** about 9 miles (15 km) long and 4 miles (7 km) wide. 2 POINTS

❸ Giotto was the name of an **Italian painter** who showed the Comet in his painting, the *Adoration of the Magi*, which depicted the birth of Jesus. 3 POINTS

❹ Halley's Comet returns **every 76 years** and will therefore be with us again in the year 2061. 3 POINTS

TOTAL SCORED ☐

Are you a GALACTIC SPACE ACE?

How did you score? Fill in your puzzle totals and add them up to find your grand total.

Puzzle 1 Total scored	Puzzle 10 Total scored ....
Puzzle 2 Total scored	Puzzle 11 Total scored ....
Puzzle 3 Total scored	Puzzle 12 Total scored ....
Puzzle 4 Total scored	Puzzle 13 Total scored ....
Puzzle 5 Total scored	Puzzle 14 Total scored ....
Puzzle 6 Total scored	Puzzle 15 Total scored ....
Puzzle 7 Total scored	Puzzle 16 Total scored ....
Puzzle 8 Total scored	Puzzle 17 Total scored ....
Puzzle 9 Total scored	Puzzle 18 Total scored ....

TOTAL ☐   TOTAL ☐

GRAND TOTAL ☐

The total number of points that you can score in this book is 160. You would be very clever indeed to get all of these.

If you scored more than 80 you are doing well. You can call yourself a GALACTIC SPACE ACE and wear the special Star-Ship Enterprise sticker.

If you scored more than 100 you did very well – you can call yourself a SPACE DOTS WIZARD.

If you scored more than 140 you must be exceptionally clever and can call yourself a SUPREME GALACTIC COMMANDER.

THANK YOUS

Eddison Sadd Editions would like to thank the following: Andrew Farmer for the illustration on the front cover; Anthony Duke and Dave Sexton for the artwork and the dots; Amanda Barlow for the design.

The following sources were used as reference for the illustrations: *Frontiers of Space* by Andrew Wilson, W H Smith, London 1985; *Manned Spacecraft* by Kenneth Gatland, Blandford Press, London 1976; *The Soviet Manned Space Programme* by Phillip Clark, Salamander Books, London 1988; *Astronomy Through the Telescope* by Richard Learner, Sceptre, London 1982; Ralph Gibbons; British Aerospace, Hatfield; and the NASA and NOVOSTI libraries.

We are especially grateful to Stewart Aviation for the loan of the badges shown on the stickers. Anyone wishing to obtain an illustrated catalogue of authentic space badges should send a large SAE and 30 pence to Stewart Aviation, PO Box 7, Market Harborough, Leicestershire, LE16 8XL.